THE BEST OF
BIRDS & BLOOMS
2013

contents

from the editor

Can you believe another year has flown by? It's been a fantastic one for *Birds & Blooms* magazine, each issue packed with eye-opening features, innovative projects and inspiring ideas from readers and experts alike. We're proud to present *The Best of Birds & Blooms 2013*, our latest collection of essential advice for birders and gardeners like you, featuring outstanding articles and photographs from the past year.

Learn how to plant a nonstop, no-fuss garden in "Garden More, Water Less" (page 124). Turn to "Big Day of Birding" (page 16) to discover how even the busiest bird-watcher can spot a record number in just 24 hours. And combine your birding and gardening skills for rewarding results in "Create the Ultimate Backyard Habitat" (page 88).

So we invite you to dig in! And once you do, we know you'll agree: *The Best of Birds & Blooms* isn't just a valuable resource, it's a beautiful keepsake you'll enjoy year after year.

Stacy Tornio

Editor, *Birds & Blooms*

create this bird feeder (page 81) in a few minutes flat!

EDITORIAL

Executive Editor/Print & Digital Books Stephen C. George
Creative Director Howard Greenberg
Editorial Services Manager Kerri Balliet

Senior Editor/Print & Digital Books Mark Hagen
Associate Editor Ellie Martin Cliffe
Associate Creative Director Edwin Robles Jr.
Art Director Raeann Sundholm
Content Production Manager Julie Wagner
Layout Designer Catherine Fletcher
Copy Chief Deb Warlaumont Mulvey
Copy Editor Dulcie Shoener
Contributing Copy Editor Valerie Phillips

Executive Editor Heather Lamb
Creative Director Sharon K. Nelson
Editor, *Birds & Blooms* Stacy Tornio
Art Director, *Birds & Blooms* Sue Myers

BUSINESS

Vice President, Publisher Russell S. Ellis
Associate Publisher Chris Dolan
New York Greg Messina, John Dyckman, Sabrina Ng, *nysales@rd.com*
Chicago Monica Thomas Kamradt, *nysales@rd.com*
West Coast Catherine Marcussen, *nysales@rd.com*
Direct Response Advertising Media People Inc.
Eric Genova, *egenova@mediapeople.com*

Travel Northeast and Southeast: Harold Chambliss,
haroldcmg@ceocenters.com
Midwest and Southwest: Jerry Greco, *jerry@jerrygreco.com*;
Susan Tauster, *susant@taustermedia.com*
West: Bob Flahive, *robertflahive@flahive.com*

Corporate Digital & Integrated Sales Director, N.A. Steve Sottile
Associate Marketing Director, Integrated Solutions Katie Gaon Wilson

Vice President, Magazine Marketing Dave Fiegel

READER'S DIGEST NORTH AMERICA

Vice President, Business Development Jonathan Bigham
President, Books and Home Entertaining Harold Clarke
Chief Financial Officer Howard Halligan
Vice President, General Manager,
Reader's Digest Media Marilynn Jacobs
Chief Marketing Officer Renee Jordan
Vice President, Chief Sales Officer Mark Josephson
General Manager, Milwaukee Frank Quigley
Vice President, Chief Content Officer Liz Vaccariello

THE READER'S DIGEST ASSOCIATION, INC.
President and Chief Executive Officer Robert E. Guth

@2013 Reiman Media Group, Inc.
5400 S. 60th St., Greendale WI 53129

International Standard Book Number (10): 1-61765-145-1
International Standard Book Number (13): 978-1-61765-145-8

International Standard Serial Number: 1553-8400

Printed in U.S.A.

1 3 5 7 9 10 8 6 4 2

Pictured on the front cover:
Monarch butterfly, Carol L. Edwards
Cedar waxwing, Maslowski Wildlife

Pictured on the back cover:
Common yellowthroat, Patty Jennings
Swallowtail, Carol Lynne Fowler
Bluebirds, Michelle Holland

CHAPTER 1

the best in Bird-Watching

Upgrade your birding skills with tips from the experts. Learn insider facts on some of America's most sought-after birds. Read all about the extraordinary experiences of backyard bird-watchers like you.

INDIGO BUNTING, RICHARD DAY / DAYBREAK IMAGERY

ultimate guide to watching

Red-breasted nuthatch

birds

Get timely tips for bird-watching no matter what season it is.

BY DAVID SHAW

Seasonality is a strange thing. Those of us who live far from the equator integrate the seasons into our lives quite naturally. We are always aware of the change of the seasons—the shifts in light and temperature, the changes in the trees, flowers and crops in our gardens. For birders, these changes are even more dramatic, as each season brings its regular species, highlights and, yes, even periods of the doldrums.

Birds adjust not only their plumage, behavior and food based on the seasons, but they also make mind-bending migrations across continents and oceans in response to them. These movements and behaviors add a dimension to the year-round changes for those of us who watch birds. Each season brings something new, something different, something that demands that we sit up and pay attention.

Waiting to Be Surprised

Winter can seem dark, cold and lifeless. Those of us who live in the northern part of the country (very far north in my case of Fairbanks, Alaska) are accustomed to snow, frigid temperatures and a landscape that can seem void of any living thing. From a birding perspective it can be monotonous. Common feeder birds flit in and out, the same few species, day in and day out. We long for the days of spring and summer.

But then, during one of our periodic glances out the window, something different appears. A pine grosbeak, perhaps, a northern shrike or a red-breasted nuthatch. The new bird flies into the branches, scattering a flurry of snow as it lands. The colors and patterns of the new arrival help us forget about the cold, the dark and the monochromatic landscape. We become entranced by the bird at hand.

This is winter birding for me in the interior of Alaska, but a similar story can be told virtually anywhere. In western Washington state, where I attended college, winter was one of the finest times of year for birding as species from across the North congregated in the wetlands and estuaries. And although there was far more diversity in those wet coastal forests than here in Alaska, one trait remained constant: Things often seemed the same, day after day.

Rain there, snow here. The species were usually the same, though there were far more of them. But the rarities and the surprises served to remind me that despite the apparent monotony, things were not always the same after all.

NUTHATCH, RICHARD DAY / DAYBREAK IMAGERY

Try to Keep Up

The pleasures of watching birds really come to light during the changes of the seasons. Wherever you live in North America, the appearance of the first migrants is a cause for celebration. It is a sign that winter has lost its grip and that the warmth of spring is not far away.

Every spring day is a bit like Christmas because there is bound to be a new gift waiting, if one is willing to look for it. In the South, the first signs of spring may not be the arrival of a new species but the sudden absence of the winter residents. Meanwhile, farther north we wait for the arrival of those same species: snow buntings, juncos, longspurs or robins. Spring is a fleeting time of sudden and constant change. It forces our attention and incites the desire to step outside, to listen and to watch.

Spring is also a time of sudden and ephemeral abundance. Weather patterns and migration occasionally coincide to create what are known as "fall-outs." Like construction on an interstate, bad weather can create a traffic jam of sorts along the migration route. Countless birds can be caught up behind the storms, waiting for their chance to move north once again. This phenomenon is particularly dramatic along the Gulf of Mexico and the Great Lakes, where flocks of migrants sometimes descend from the sky, decorating the shrubs and trees like colorful, living ornaments.

Migration, of course, is not always so dramatic. Often it is as simple as backyards, recently silent, newly filled with the sounds of birds. Not all species arrive at the same time. The sparrows are often first, heralding the arrival of others. Birds arrive one species after another until the last wave of wings has flowed north up the continent.

Flurry of Activity

When the blasts of heat arrive with summer, the birds change their tunes. They, like us, settle into a routine. Summer, so different from winter in many respects, surprisingly bears some similarities.

It can be a time of apparent stagnation. But, unlike the cold months, it is the stagnation of a tropical lake. Still, yes, but filled with expanding life as nests are constructed, eggs laid and hatched, nestlings fed and eventually fledged. The species may not change all that much, but the birds are boisterous and multiplying.

The mottled browns and streaky plumage of the first juvenile sparrows challenge the identification skills of the most astute birder. Then, as observers get a grasp on the sparrows, fledgling warblers and flycatchers appear, and the challenge begins anew. Confusing us more, adult birds look worn and tattered, like the tired parents they are, and seem to sulk in the brush, exhausted. For a few weeks in July and August the trees are again filled, as fledglings disperse and adults start to fuel up for the molt into their winter plumage and the migration to follow.

One day in September a species or two goes missing. Like a partygoer who attends out of politeness or obligation, the last species to arrive is often the first to leave. Here in Alaska, the alder flycatcher, a species that spends only around six weeks on the breeding grounds, is the first to flee the North and start its journey to the far southern portion of South America. Soon another species follows, then another and another.

By early September, in my neck of the woods, there is a veritable flurry of fluttering wings as one after another the migrants pick up and fly south, the first tendrils of winter brushing their retreating tails. As winter again grabs control of the landscape, left behind is a small cluster of resident birds breathing a sigh of relief as they reclaim the forests, fields and backyard feeders as their own.

WEATHER PATTERNS. Weather plays a large role in bird activity. If a storm comes through, it can affect birds for thousands of miles. Below, American robins often travel together in winter because it's easier to find food. At left are a robin's nest hidden among spring azalea blooms and an eastern phoebe in summer.

for less

Have fun in your backyard with these no-cost ideas.

family nest watch

OPEN WIDE. Keep a watchful eye on a nest and you might witness a parent feeding its young, as in this family of cedar waxwings.

Keeping an eye on the birds that nest near you in the summer is a terrific family activity, and it doesn't cost a thing. Use these tips to get the most out of this *free* entertainment!

LOOK FOR NEST CAMS. Online nest cams get a lot of attention in spring, but don't forget that nesting season lasts all summer. There's still a lot of action at many of those nests, or there might be another brood going already. Check out your favorites to follow the progress of nesting bird stars.

KEEP A JOURNAL. Chronicle the development of the young in your yard by observing, tracking and writing every day. Then next year, you can pull out your journal and see how the growth compares.

PHOTOGRAPH THE PROCESS. Don't get close enough to disturb the nest, but carefully, quietly get your shots. Robins, for instance, are fun to photograph through the whole process of nest building, egg laying and raising their young.

GO ON A NEST HUNT. Whether you have nests in your own backyard or not, it's fun to look around to see what you find. Take a pair of binoculars. Look high and low, and see what you can spot.

WATCH FOR JUVENILES. Many young birds can be mistaken for adults, but observe them for a while and you may find them looking around for guidance or feeding. Once you spot one, it's a joy to watch it discovering the world.

the
songsters
of summer

Vireos are tough to spot, but their delightfully
persistent singing makes them worth finding.

BY KENN AND KIMBERLY KAUFMAN

YELLOW-THROATED.
To glimpse the yellow-throated vireo, look up! Like other vireos, they prefer to stay high in the treetops.

Among songbirds, vireos often play second fiddle to more colorful families such as warblers, orioles and buntings. And we might say they have themselves to blame.

Small birds with big voices, masters of subtlety, vireos are like songbirds in stealth mode. Their modest plumage and habit of foraging in dense foliage can make them quite a challenge to see. Fortunately, they're among our continent's most persistent singers, making themselves heard in spring and summer all over North America.

Subtle Beauty

The word "vireo" comes from the Latin for "green." Most vireos are predominantly olive-green or gray. A few, such as the yellow-throated vireo and blue-headed vireo, sport brighter tones. Out of the roughly 14 vireo species in North America, most fall into one of two pattern types: with wing bars and eye rings, or with plain wings and pale eyebrow stripes.

To call vireos persistent singers is actually an understatement. During nesting season, the red-eyed vireo of the Eastern forests will start singing half an hour before sunrise and will continue, almost without a break, until late afternoon. Its song is a series of short phrases: *See-chevit, sisi-chweet, chyew-chi-swee, syew-sip*—on and on, with only a second or two between songs.

It may sing dozens of songs per minute, a few thousand in an hour or tens of thousands in a day. It will sing even through the heat of the summer day when other birds have fallen silent.

One scientist—with a persistence that could only be described as vireolike—analyzed 12,500 different song types from red-eyed vireos. He then pointed out that this was only a sample, not a complete inventory!

Singing From the Cradle

In most species of vireos, the male and female take turns sitting on the nest to incubate the eggs. This doesn't necessarily mean a long interruption in the male's singing, however, because male vireos may sing even while sitting on the nest. A male blue-headed vireo, for example, often will incubate silently at first, but if his mate doesn't come back soon enough to relieve him of nest duty, he will start to sing.

There's little danger that the singing male will give away the nest's location to lurking predators, however. A vireo nest is well-camouflaged: simply a small cup of plant fibers suspended in the fork of a twig. It may not be completely surrounded by foliage, but it's almost always in a shady spot, often difficult to see from the ground.

Blue-headed

Bell's

Red-eyed

Warbling

Hutton's

Food Habits

During spring and summer, vireos are mostly insect eaters. They seem methodical, even sluggish, as they hop about in trees or shrubs, seeking caterpillars, beetles or other morsels.

But the sluggishness disappears when a vireo nabs a large, active insect: The bird will thrash its prey against a branch over and over to subdue it. The tip of a vireo's bill has a small hook on the upper mandible, reminiscent of the hooked bill of a bird of prey, undoubtedly useful in handling large insects.

Vireos are among those birds whose diet may change with the seasons. In late summer, they begin to feed on berries, such as those of dogwoods and elderberries, or wild grapes. Some vireos, including the blue-headed, white-eyed and Hutton's, may spend the winter in warmer parts of the U.S., but others go to the tropics. For example, red-eyed vireos take red-eye flights to South America, where they may feed mostly on small fruits in winter.

Attracting Vireos

How do you attract vireos to your yard? They don't nest in birdhouses, and they don't come to bird feeders. Water will attract them, especially a birdbath with a dripper or a trickle of water placed reasonably close to leafy cover. And they may come to eat the fruits of native dogwoods in late summer or early fall.

The best way to entice these sweet singers is to encourage the growth of native trees and shrubs in your landscape. Also, avoid pesticides that kill the caterpillars and other insects that vireos feast upon.

Even if vireos are not the most colorful of birds, you can enhance your appreciation of them by learning their songs, their plumage and their habits. Get to know these accomplished musicians of the avian world, and you may discover hidden treasures in your foliage.

5 interesting vireo songs

BELL'S VIREO: Answers its own question with *Cheedle cheedle chee? Cheedle cheedle chew!*

YELLOW-THROATED VIREO: A hoarse song of *Zeeyoo—breeyoowit—wheeyay* and so on.

HUTTON'S VIREO: A simple repeating call of *Zuwee? Zuwee? Zuwee?*

WHITE-EYED VIREO (shown): An explosive call that sounds like advice to the guys: *Pick up a real chick!*

WARBLING VIREO: A rapid song that some ornithologists suggest sounds like: *If I see it I will seize it, I will squeeze it till it squirts!*

BIG

day of birding

Don't have time for a Big Year? Learn how to master a day instead.

BY KEN KEFFER

Excitement, adventure, competition and fun—it's all in a day's work.

In 2011, a movie called *The Big Year* starring comedy giants Steve Martin, Owen Wilson and Jack Black put birding's biggest competition in the spotlight, portraying the scramble to find as many species as possible in a single calendar year. But what about the rest of us?

Most of us don't have the time or the money to take on a Big Year. Last spring I was so busy I opted for a Big Half-Hour instead!

Maybe a single day is more your style. A Big Day can be as simple as counting the birds in your backyard. Or, like many others, you might choose to take your adventure on the road, putting together a team and counting as many species as you can in 24 hours.

Remember, this is your Big Day, so you can define the pursuit as you see fit. You can even go green by tallying only species you find on foot, by bicycle or via public transportation. Here are a few tips to make your experience a memorable one.

Plan Your Route

The key to finding the most bird species is to visit diverse habitats. However, time spent behind the wheel is rarely the most productive for finding birds. You need to find the right balance between birding the hot spots where you'll find lots of species, and traveling to specialty habitats where a limited number of unusual birds might be.

A veteran of more than 20 Big Days in four states, Jessie Barry notes the importance of having a plan early on. In particular, figure out the best place to spend sunrise, that magic hour when all sorts of species can be seen or at least heard.

"Dawn is often an incredible, mind-boggling experience as you listen to the birds wake up," she says, so be sure not to leave your sunrise location to chance.

Scout Ahead of Time

You'll see more birds on your Big Day if you put some effort into research beforehand. With the click of a mouse, you can learn about all kinds of recent sightings in your area.

Scouting out a rare bird in advance can save precious minutes during the Big Day. Many local species can be surprisingly elusive, so having a couple of areas staked out for them can really pay off.

Birds to find:
- Great Horned Owl
- Mallard Duck
- Sandhill Crane
- Plover
- Eastern Bluebird
- Red Winged Blackbird
- Pelican
- Chipping Sparrow

seashore

forest

Wetland

Meadow

Be Flexible

If you want to meticulously plan out a route beforehand, by all means go right ahead. But if living in the moment is more your style, roll with it. One thing to keep in mind, though: Never feel locked in to your plans. Each day is different, especially during migration season.

Flocks of finches, flycatchers and warblers may have been crowding the park just days before, but if the birds aren't around when you're working an area, you might have to make the call to move on. That said, don't give in to the grass-is-always-greener mentality. There's a fine line between the urgency of a Big Day and running around like a sage grouse with its head cut off.

Don't Forget the Snacks

While you can make time to eat an occasional meal during a Big Year, there's often no such luxury during a Big Day. Some folks justify a lunch stop as a chance to tally feeder birds, but others prefer to get their calories on the go.

Personally, my enthusiasm is fueled by coffee and lots of snacks throughout the day. Whatever your vice, don't forget to pack plenty to keep you going.

Pace Yourself

Perhaps you have a diurnal Big Day crew. Or maybe you're in it for the long haul, a midnight-to-midnight push. Either way, Big Days are surprisingly strenuous. For me, the anticipation and excitement of finding a new species to tally keeps me going all day. But everyone is different, and you have to plan according to your strengths.

Jessie's intensity kicks up a notch during the final hours of daylight. "It's often a make-or-break time," she says. "A couple of hours after the sun goes down, I'm usually overwhelmed

Great Horned Owl

by fatigue, but then it's time to rally to rack up a few more rails or owls."

Bird for a Cause

Many Big Days are held as birdathon fundraisers—they are a bit like a walkathon, but the money pledged is for each species tallied instead of every mile walked.

Jessie, for instance, often birds for the Cornell Lab of Ornithology's Team Sapsucker. Every year, the team raises more than $200,000 to support the programs the lab faciliates.

You can do something similar, using the opportunity to benefit a favorite bird observatory or local nature center. You'll discover that it is very rewarding to support conservation efforts while doing something you love.

Have Fun

Sure, there can be competition during a Big Day. You might be up against other teams vying for the top spot, or maybe you're hoping to find more species than you have in previous years. But really, the event is supposed to be fun.

Appreciating birds is what it's all about! That and the camaraderie truly keep me coming back to such events time and again.

No matter what, however, always remember there's no right or wrong way to do it. Just get out there and seize the Big Day.

voices of experience

Paul

Jessie

Malkolm

Kayla

They've all done either Big Days or Big Years, so we asked them for a little advice. Here's what they had to say:

"Each Big Day holds a memory of something exciting you wouldn't have experienced if you weren't out there in the field all day."

JESSIE BARRY, *Cornell Lab of Ornithology's Big Day team*

"At least for me, a Big Year starts with the birds and ends with the people. You love getting new birds but spend more time chatting with all the other twitchers."

PAUL RISS, *Punk Rock Big Year*

"Most birders can't take a year off and ride their bikes across the continent in search of birds like I did, but there are many ways that birders can be more climate-friendly. Try birding closer to home. Or you can walk, bike or carpool instead of driving."

MALKOLM BOOTHROYD, *who cycled more than 13,000 miles for a Big Year with his parents*

"I've done both a Big Day and a Big Sit (you sit in a hot spot and count birds for several hours), and I wouldn't hesitate to do them again. I love getting to bird with others who share a similar passion."

KAYLA PARRY, *Ohio Young Birders Club*

famous BIRDERS

BY ANN WILSON

birding advice from the pros

Alongside every great bird man, there's a great bird woman. OK, not always. But for the birding pairs here, it's absolutely true. Meet these famous duos—and get their top tips for bringing more birds to your place.

george & kit harrison

Readers of this magazine know George's "Glad You Asked" feature, but they may not know that he was one of the founding editors of *Birds & Blooms*. He says his interest in all things avian began when his parents pushed his crib against a window so he could watch the birds. Growing up, he traveled all over the country with his dad, a wildlife writer and photographer. He followed in his dad's footsteps, and now he says he can't imagine doing anything else. **GEORGE'S OTHER HALF:** Kit Harrison has been with George for 36 years. She edits all his writing. Together, they've produced 13 books and have worked on six PBS specials. Take a look at their top birding tips…

" Feeders are very important, but if you don't have natural cover, preferably native, at all levels, you won't have much bird variety. The best plants provide both food and cover, so think about options that also produce berries, seed or nectar. **—GEORGE** "

Make sure you wear the right gear. A few years ago I discovered insect-repellent clothing. It really works. **—KIT**

kenn & kimberly kaufman

Kenn has been interested in birds since age 6. At 16, he left high school and hitchhiked across the country in a quest to identify as many birds as possible in one year. He found an amazing 666 of them; his book *Kingbird Highway* chronicles the adventure. Today he has a field guide series and is one of the top pros in North America. But for someone who's seen every bird on the continent but one, the whiskered auklet, he's surprisingly unconcerned with numbers. He just loves birding, no matter what it is.

KENN'S OTHER HALF: Kimberly Kaufman is also a birding professional, working as executive director of the Black Swamp Bird Observatory in Ohio. She's always had a passion for birds and the outdoors and, like Kenn, writes for *Birds & Blooms*. They offer up this advice…

> " Identifying birds can be learned with a little practice. Ask yourself how you'd identify a common " bird if it had no markings or color. How is the bird sitting? What's its shape? How is it moving and behaving? Studying birds you already know will help you to identify more unusual birds when they do show up. **—KENN**

Share your love of birds with family and friends. The joy that birds bring to our lives is such an amazing gift. Don't keep it to yourself! **—KIMBERLY**

jim & nancy carpenter

Jim opened the first Wild Birds Unlimited store in Indianapolis more than 30 years ago. The franchise company now consists of more than 270 independently owned stores, each devoted to backyard birders. As a kid, Jim excitedly watched hummingbirds at his grandmother's home in rural Indiana. Joining an Audubon group in college rekindled that boyhood interest.

JIM'S OTHER HALF: Nancy Carpenter, a former teacher, has applied many of her classroom skills to help Jim expand their business. Nancy has worked in many areas of the company. While she is a backyard bird enthusiast, Jim says she's not "crazy like I am." See what you learn…

" Everyone has a different feeding situation. For some, a big hopper feeder is best. For others, it might be better to put a little food in a tray feeder each day when it's time to watch the birds. To attract a wide variety of birds, provide diverse food in a variety of feeders. —JIM "

Take care of your birds. To keep them from flying into the glass and injuring themselves, hang ribbons in front of the windows so they flutter in the wind. —NANCY

ADVICE FROM BIRDERS. Use the tips provided by these famous birders to attract and see fliers like cedar waxwings (pictured here) and indigo buntings (previous spread).

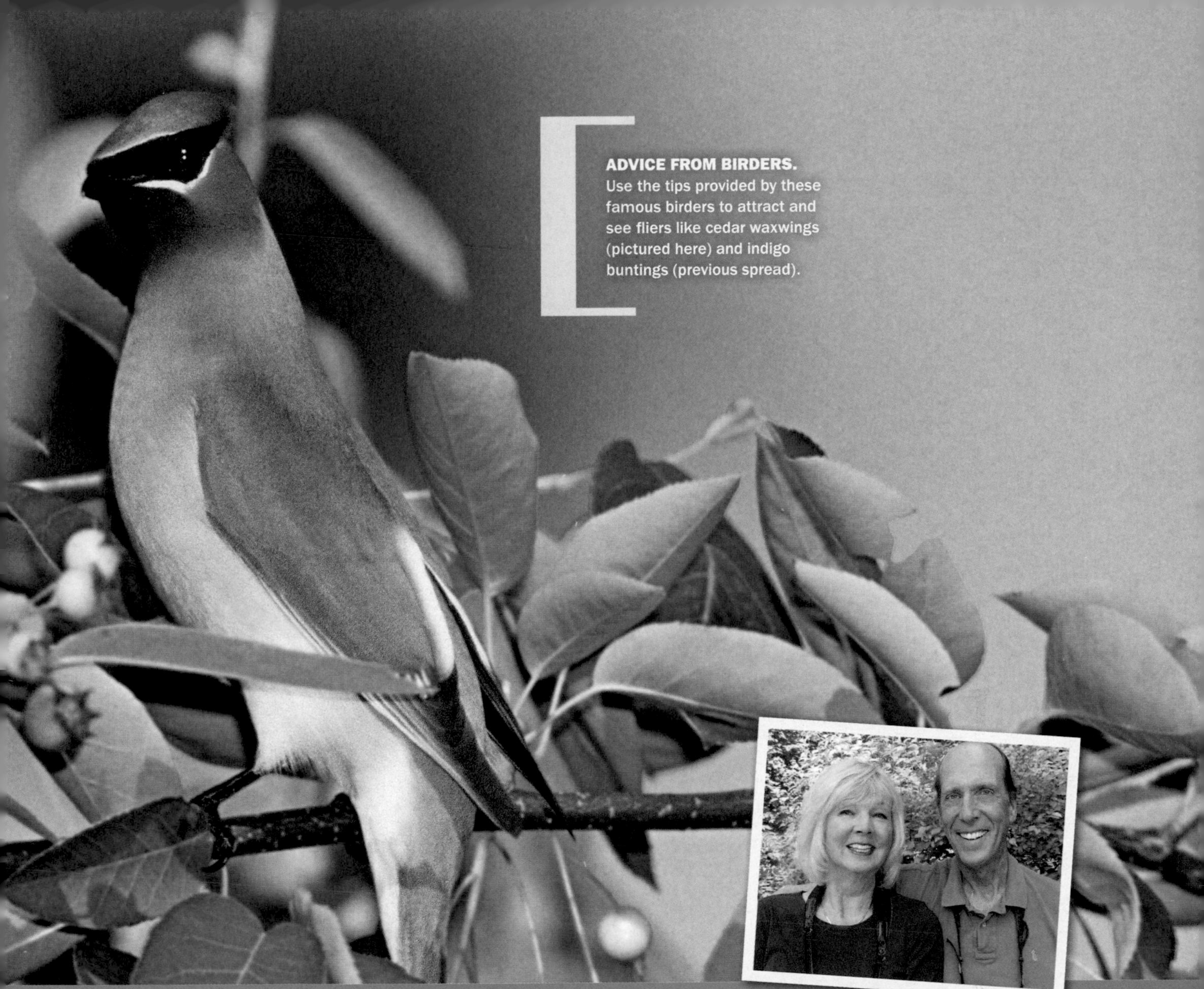

donald & lillian stokes

You can't talk about Donald Stokes without mentioning Lillian at the same time. They just might be America's best-known birding couple. Together they've written 32 bird books and have hosted several PBS and DIY Network series on the subject—and they say they couldn't have done any of it alone. They naturally go together. Lillian met Don more than 30 years ago, when she took his birding class, and they've been together ever since. They now live on 48 acres in New Hampshire, where they have identified 195 species of birds. Here are their tips…

“Use binoculars to watch your feeder birds, and don't underestimate what you can learn from birds there. For instance, if you watch consistently and closely, it's possible to see goldfinches' entire molting process when they visit your feeder. **—DON**

Pull out all the stops in your backyard. Try everything—different foods in different feeders in different places. Provide plenty of perching spots by propping up large dead tree limbs near your feeders where all sorts of birds can easily perch. **—LILLIAN**”

Tanager Treat

I had the surprise of my birding life when this beautiful western tanager showed up in my backyard last year in mid-May. I had never seen one before, so it was a rare treat. It loved the grape jelly and orange halves that I put out for the orioles.

MONA DOEBLER, *Hinsdale, Montana*

Patio Prisoner

When my 9-year-old son, Ethan, took me to our screened-in patio to help a trapped bird, I imagined a curious downy woodpecker or little chickadee. Instead, I was shocked to find a juvenile red-tailed hawk, flapping all around.

Slowly, I stepped into the room, speaking quietly to the bird as it hopped around and continued assaulting the screen. It paused, and I saw it looked tired, so I bent and placed my hands around its wings, gently pinning them to its body. It slowly rotated its head around to look at me, and I winced, expecting squawking, maybe an attack. But it remained calm, allowing me to carefully walk it outside.

In the backyard, I told my wife and son that this was something we would probably never get to see again. Then I pointed the bird toward the trees, held it high and released my grip.

The hawk stretched its wings, which spanned about 3 feet, and rose majestically into the air, soaring toward a thicket. We watched in awe of the experience we had just shared. Of course, that's when I thought about a camera.

MICHAEL SGRIGNOLI
Middletown, Pennsylvania

Dip-a-Dee-Dee-Dee! ▶

These chickadees perched on the hummingbird feeder, chattering to each other and showing interest in the sugar water. Suddenly, one dived right in and started drinking. They were so funny, standing on their heads for a sweet sip.

ANNE ZENESKI
Raleigh, North Carolina

I'm almost to the good stuff!

▼ Funny-Looking Dogs

On a drive through South Dakota's Badlands National Park with my daughter and grandchildren, we kept an eye out for prairie dogs. About halfway through the park, I thought I saw a few, although they were far away, so we pulled over to watch. The grandchildren were excited and competed for window space. Just as my daughter and I were commenting on our luck, 3-year-old Scarlett said, "Mommy, those prairie dogs look like birdies."

I reached for my camera and telephoto lens and looked through the viewfinder. Sure enough—what we thought were prairie dogs turned out to be a family of burrowing owls. We spent the better part of an hour watching them and snapping photos. We saw plenty of prairie dogs that trip, but no more burrowing owls.

KATHY ROWLAND
Mattoon, Illinois

Christmas Cardinal ▶

Our 4-year-old granddaughter, Molly, asked us for a bird feeder. We gave her one of our extras but explained that it might take her a little time to attract the birds because they don't always find new feeders right away.

Only two days later, though, Molly spotted a cardinal at the feeder and called us to say, "He's beautiful!" Maybe the red bows helped get his attention. We're thrilled that she had almost instant success.

PAUL & JOANNE BUEGE
Watertown, Wisconsin

won over by

Yellow warbler

warblers

It takes a little extra effort to spot these gorgeous birds, but you won't be disappointed.

BY KENN AND KIMBERLY KAUFMAN

Common yellowthroat

Watching warblers in spring is like being invited to a secret festival. These colorful, fascinating little creatures, often called the butterflies of the bird world, are among our favorite fliers.

The average person has probably never seen a warbler. They are fast and tiny birds that seem to spend most of their time hiding in treetops, singing soft, high-pitched songs. But once you're tuned in to these vibrant birds, you're sure to become a member of the warbler fan club!

A Diverse and Colorful Family

More than 50 species of warblers are found regularly in North America, north of the Mexican border. They average no more than 5 inches from the tip of the bill to the tip of the tail, and most weigh less than half an ounce. All feed primarily on tiny insects.

Perhaps the best thing about warblers is that most of them boast bright colors, sharp patterns or both. Warblers make up a dazzling galaxy of yellow, green, blue, orange and other colors, with accents of black and white. Yes, they may be challenging to see, but their snappy good looks make them worth the effort.

During their summer nesting season, different species of warblers go to different habitats. Blackburnian warblers and blackpoll warblers go to spruce forests of the North, prothonotary warblers seek out Southern swamps, and black-throated gray warblers spend the summer in the oak and juniper woodlands of Western foothills. But during their spring and fall migration, many of them overlap. A single location might host more than 30 species. Spring is ideal for warbler watching because they're sporting such colorful plumage, so it's definitely the time to get outside!

Tiny Travelers

All of our North American warblers are at least partly migratory, moving to warmer climates in fall, with some traveling thousands of miles. The vast majority go to the tropics for the winter, including Mexico and Central America, Caribbean islands or even northern South America. These are impressive feats for birds weighing less than an ounce.

When they come back north in spring, they seem to bring tropical color and warmth with them. Their arrival is

Cerulean warbler

Northern parula

Blackburnian warbler

A Front-Row Seat for the Parade

So how do you go about finding warblers? Watch for these tiny birds making short, quick movements in the trees. And while warblers don't usually come to feeders, they may visit birdbaths placed close to trees. If you find one warbler, be sure to look around for others, because they often travel in small, mixed flocks.

There are also concentration points where sheer numbers make them easier to see. In inland regions, trees along rivers through open country may host good numbers of transient warblers. City parks along the Gulf Coast, in places like Galveston, Texas, and St. Petersburg, Florida, are sometimes hopping with warblers that have just crossed the Gulf. Many spots around the Great Lakes are exceptionally good for migrant warblers, as the birds pause there before or after crossing the water.

We're lucky enough to live in northwestern Ohio, on the shores of Lake Erie, known as "The Warbler Capital of the World" because of the huge number of the birds that stop here in May.

When spring comes around, make sure you watch for the warbler parade and introduce yourself to these delightful birds. They may be tiny, but they deliver a lot of color and personality in a small package. Get to know these feathered gems and add a taste of the tropics to your garden or your favorite birding hot spot!

like a parade, except that it goes on for weeks and involves millions of participants. From coast to coast, warblers sweep northward across all of North America. In the lower 48 states, warblers could literally visit any tree during their spring migration.

The parade will vary from place to place, because different kinds of warblers come from different wintering grounds and head to different destinations. Some species, like the black-throated blue warbler and the Cape May warbler, spend the winter in the Caribbean, so they make their way north mostly by going through Florida, fanning out as they go.

Others, such as the Nashville and Wilson's warblers, spend the winter mostly in Mexico, so their parade route brings them through the western end of the Gulf of Mexico.

Many warblers that winter farther to the south and east in Mexico or Central America, such as the magnolia, chestnut-sided, golden-winged and bay-breasted species, will come up through the Yucatan Peninsula and then fly straight north across the Gulf of Mexico, arriving on our Gulf Coast at any point between eastern Texas and western Florida.

The point is, any part of the U.S. has the potential for warblers. Wherever you live, you're on the route!

victories

Birds are beating all odds and making comebacks, thanks to these conservation efforts.

BY KENN AND KIMBERLY KAUFMAN

in BIRDING

We all love success stories, especially when they're about birds! Wouldn't it be great if each of us could be part of the stories, helping to write a chapter or two in the annals of bird conservation? Changing the birding world might seem like a daunting goal, but it starts with small steps that practically anyone can take. Here are some of our favorite examples of birding success stories over the years. We hope they inspire you!

Boxes for Bluebirds

They are among America's best-loved birds, but that wasn't enough to keep our three species of bluebirds out of trouble early in the 20th century. The natural tree cavities they needed for nest sites were becoming scarcer, and competition for those sites—from introduced starlings and house sparrows—was edging the bluebirds out.

Fortunately, bluebirds will readily adopt manmade birdhouses, or nest boxes. In recent decades, armies of bluebird fans have put up nest boxes by the hundreds of thousands, perhaps even the millions. Some people may set up one or two boxes on a small property, while more ambitious devotees run "bluebird trails" with dozens of boxes installed along miles of country roads.

Maintaining such trails is a lot of work, but the results have been outstanding. Surveys over the past four decades show that mountain bluebird populations have been holding steady, while numbers of eastern bluebirds and western bluebirds have been increasing. It's good news for the birds and good news for anyone who appreciates natural beauty.

The Duck Stamp

What if, for an investment of just $15, you could be part of a program that has conserved more than 6 million acres of bird habitat? What if your $15 investment also brought you an exquisite small piece of collectible art? This is not only possible but easy as well, and you can do it every year by buying the federal Duck Stamp. (The one pictured here is from 1934.)

The official name of this little item is the Migratory Bird Hunting and Conservation Stamp. When the stamp was introduced in 1934, it served mainly as a hunting license, but it has grown into far more than that. Each stamp design is chosen in a contest that attracts top artists. Volunteer judges (Kenn was a judge one year) select from among hundreds of entries, and the winning design goes on the next year's stamp. The program itself is so efficient that about $14.70 of each $15 stamp goes directly into buying wetland habitat, and this habitat supports not only ducks but also herons, grebes, rails, wrens and many other birds. More and more bird-watchers are buying these Duck Stamps every year. Learn more at *fws.gov/duckstamps*.

FOR THE BIRDS. Bluebird populations are up because of caring birders. Put up a house today to help make a difference.

U.S. DEPARTMENT OF AGRICULTURE

VOID AFTER JUNE 30, 1935

ONE DOLLAR

MIGRATORY BIRD HUNTING STAMP

ONE DOLLAR

Eagles Everywhere

John Denver sang, "I know he'd be a poorer man if he never saw an eagle fly." Once your life has been graced by the sight of an eagle, you'll be all the better for it. When many eyes are watching eagles, it can be great for the birds, too.

Just a few years ago, bald eagles were in serious trouble. Poisoned by certain pesticides, the adults in many nests were laying eggs that never hatched. Even after the most damaging pesticides were banned, numbers were slow to recover. In our state of Ohio, for example, only two pairs remained in the late 1970s.

To give the birds their best chance at recovery, state wildlife agencies across the U.S. set up programs for citizen volunteers to monitor nesting pairs of eagles. Kimberly volunteered for Ohio's Division of Wildlife in the 1990s, spending days looking through a telescope to observe nest activity and watch for any danger to the birds.

Thousands of eagle monitors across the country played a part in the spectacular comeback of the bald eagle. Here in Ohio, for example, the number of nesting pairs has grown from two to more than 250! More and more Americans now can thrill to the sight of an eagle in flight.

Coffee Made in the Shade

Picture a lush forest in the American tropics. As we look about, we see birds everywhere—not just tropical birds but also migratory birds from North America, including tanagers, orioles, warblers and others. Looking down at the forest floor, we realize that the dappled shade is falling on coffee plants. This is a working coffee farm; it is also a fine habitat for birds.

The coffee we drink can have an impact on birds. Coffee grown the traditional way—organically, in the shade of native trees—has benefits for all involved. Under these conditions, coffee farms provide jobs in local communities, produce superior-tasting coffee and offer habitat for resident and migratory birds.

We recently surveyed one such farm in Nicaragua and were moved by the dedication of the people and the abundance of birds in this habitat. Look for the Smithsonian Migratory Bird Center's Bird Friendly seal (at right) to be sure your coffee really is good for the birds!

Going Native

Lady Bird Johnson once said that native plants "give us a sense of where we are in this great land of ours."

THEY'RE BACK. Bald eagles are no longer in trouble. The number of nesting pairs has grown significantly since the 1970s.

Just as important, native plants also support native birds and butterflies. But people often choose garden and landscape plants purely on the basis of their looks, without any regard to whether they are natives or not. As a result, vast areas of gardens, yards and parks may look attractive to humans but have minimal value to birds or other wildlife.

Fortunately, there's a growing movement toward gardening with native plants. This movement gives us a chance to discover things about our natural heritage. For gardeners with busy lives, native plants have the added advantage of requiring less watering and maintenance than non-natives, since they are already adapted to the climate of the area. As more and more people take up the joys of gardening with natives, growing numbers of native birds can thrive in our towns and cities.

These are just a few examples. You may find many other possibilities by contacting local organizations, such as nature centers or conservation groups. The important thing to remember is that all of us can take small steps that add up to big differences for birds.

Northern mockingbird

Long Live the Birds

BY GEORGE HARRISON

Take a look at some of your favorite backyard birds and their expected longevity. You might be surprised at what you find.

The first year of a wild bird's life is the toughest. Some research shows that 80 percent of songbirds live no longer than a year. It's hard to imagine that most of those fledglings you see in your backyard aren't going to be around very long.

According to a study by Stanley Temple, a professor of forest and wildlife ecology at the University of Wisconsin-Madison, 40 percent of black-capped chickadees do not survive their first year, and the average life span of the species in the wild is about 2½ years. Yet the potential longevity of a black-capped chickadee is more than 12 years. Predators, severe weather, food shortages, accidents and disease make it difficult for birds to enjoy a double-digit life span.

My guess is that the average backyard songbird, if it survives its first year, lives between three and five years. However, it should be noted that birds in captivity usually live longer than their counterparts in the wild.

In general, larger birds enjoy longer lives. Eagles, condors and owls have been known to live more than 40 years in the wild. One great horned owl reportedly lived 68 years, while a swan is said to have reached the age of 102.

So the outlook may seem dismal, but there is some hope for birds to live a long life. Take a look at some of the longest-lived birds on record, all identified through banding efforts from the U.S. Geological Survey.

Northern cardinal: 13½
Northern mockingbird: 12
American robin: 11½
European starling: 16
Red-bellied woodpecker: 20½
Common grackle: 16

EAGLES, MICHIO HOSHINO / MINDEN PICTURES; MOCKINGBIRD, SARI ONEAL / SHUTTERSTOCK.COM

Alaska's
extraordinary

Remarkable birds travel thousands of miles to reach their breeding grounds each year.

BY DAVID SHAW

IMPRESSIVE MIGRANTS.
Arctic terns (pictured here) travel more than 36,000 miles in a single year for migration between breeding and wintering grounds.

MIGRANTS

Most people imagine Alaska as a mountainous and cold landscape, isolated in the far north, wild and alone. I see a wild and beautiful landscape, indeed, but one connected by birds to the rest of the world. No, Alaska is not isolated; I think it's actually the center of the bird world.

Alaska's wild landscapes and intact habitats regularly lure birds from six of the world's continents. Six—all but Europe! That's practically the entire planet. Few places can boast that kind of geographic diversity in bird life, and it is one of the reasons I live here. And the birds themselves are even more impressive than their diversity. To fly between Alaska and their wintering grounds, some species take on migrations that are unparalleled—and nearly incomprehensible.

Dozens of species, many of them familiar winter feeder birds in the Lower 48, spend their summers in the far north. Slate-colored junco (the all-gray subspecies of dark-eyed junco) is one. White-crowned sparrow is another. Yellow-rumped warbler is a third. The list goes on. Take a look at some more of the most impressive summer visitors in Alaska.

Slate-colored junco

White-crowned sparrow

Yellow-rumped warbler

Worldly Travelers

South America hosts a substantial number of Alaska's birds. Swainson's and gray-cheeked thrushes, blackpoll warblers and numerous shorebirds, from the diminutive Baird's sandpiper to the stately whimbrel, find their way into the fields, forests and wild coasts of South America.

The blackpoll warbler, weighing a mere 12 grams in the summer, has a jaw-dropping southern migration. This little bird departs its breeding grounds in the boreal forests and tundra of interior Alaska and heads not south, but east— all the way to Canada's Atlantic coast, where it pauses and eats. And eats, and eats. This bird packs on fat until it reaches the avian equivalent of obesity, more than doubling its normal body weight.

Then, carrying all that stored fuel, it takes flight from the northeast coast and heads out over the churning waves of the Atlantic. With no place to stop, no rest, no food, the blackpoll flaps its wings ceaselessly for more than three days. Eventually, nearly starved, it arrives on the northern coast of South America.

Another one of my favorite summer Alaska birds is the tiny, greenish-yellow arctic warbler. Though similar in appearance, it's unrelated to the familiar wood warblers of North and South America. Rather, it's primarily an Old World species more closely related to thrushes. In Alaska, these warblers breed in the shrubby willow tundra of the mountainous interior and north. Wherever arctic warblers are found during the breeding season, an exquisite view of wild, rugged mountains is guaranteed. However, during winter, these birds choose quite a different setting as they migrate across the Bering Strait and south along the eastern coast of Asia as far south as the hot and humid rain forests of the Philippines.

Familiar Faces Far Away

A few years ago, I worked as a naturalist-guide on a small cruise ship in the Southern Ocean. We were among the icebergs, penguin colonies and towering glaciers of the Antarctic Peninsula when the butterfly-like flight of a tern caught my eye. *Hmm,* I thought to myself, *that looks a lot like an arctic tern.* And it was. The same species that breeds along ponds and rivers in my home state during the summer patrols the glaciated coast of the Antarctic Peninsula when it's winter in Alaska. Traveling the world, it crisscrosses oceans and continents twice, flying more than 36,000 miles every single year.

The mountainous tundra of western Alaska is the only place in North America where you can find the bar-tailed godwit, a pigeon-sized shorebird with a long, slightly upturned bill and thinly striped tail. They are beautiful birds, but it's their remarkable autumn migration that sets them apart.

With the arrival of fall, the godwits move down from the mountains to the coast of western Alaska, where they wait and feed. When a weather system spirals in just the right location in the North Pacific, they set off. Propelled by

Bar-tailed godwit

strong winds, the birds fly out over the ocean, west at first, and then due south.

About three days later they pass somewhere near Hawaii and the tiny islands of the South Pacific, but they don't stop. Onward they fly, without rest, food or water—flapping, flapping, as thousands of miles of open ocean pass beneath their wings. Finally, nearly a week after their departure from the Alaska coast, the exhausted and emaciated bar-tailed godwits alight on the beaches of New Zealand and Australia, safe on their wintering grounds.

A Long Commute

The high ridges and mountainsides of interior and northern Alaska's low, rocky tundra provide a summer home for a strange, thrush-size, black-and-gray songbird. At first glance the northern wheatear resembles a mockingbird or shrike. But unlike those species, the wheatear lives a more eccentric lifestyle. While I'm accustomed to hearing its chattering songs on summer hikes in the mountains north of my home in Fairbanks, it sings in a quite different place during Alaska's winter.

With the arrival of fall, the wheatears I've been watching fly west. They pass over the Bering Strait and into far eastern Russia. From there they head southwest, across Siberia, central Asia, the Middle East and Turkey. Next, they continue across the Mediterranean, over the coast of northern Africa and the blowing sands of the Sahara. Finally, they settle upon the game-rich grasslands of Kenya and Tanzania, where they spend their winter amongst giraffes, zebras, elephants and lions. Imagine this: caribou and grizzly bears in the summer, leopards and wildebeest in the winter. It doesn't get much more diverse than that.

Horned grebe

common wanderers
These birds spend summers in Alaska, but you might see them in your area during winter.

Ring-necked duck

Common loon

Horned grebe

Golden-crowned sparrow

White-crowned sparrow

Dark-eyed junco

Orange-crowned warbler

Yellow-rumped warbler

American pipit

American tree sparrow

Common redpoll

Common loon

American pipit

Ring-necked duck

birding
glad you asked!

Backyard Bird-Watcher George Harrison is here to answer your toughest questions!

▼ Set the Record Straight

Can you tell me whether the photo below is a purple finch or a house finch? How can you tell?

KYLE IASIELLO, *Walnutport, Pennsylvania*

George: This is a male purple finch. Many people have difficulty distinguishing between male purple finches and male house finches. The most significant differences are the shape of the bill, the location of the red feathers, and the shade and amount of red.

The bill is thicker and more conical in purple finches, and much more sharp and pointed in house finches. The purple finch is a deeper red, almost a raspberry, while the house finch is more of a strawberry red. The male purple finch has red all over its head, breast, back and the tops of its wings, while the house finch is brown on the back and wings.

Impressive Nest Builder

We recently bought some wooded property in southern Illinois. While taking a walk, we noticed a pouchlike nest hanging high in a cottonwood tree. What kind of bird might have built this interesting nest?

DEBBIE DEMENT, *DuQuoin, Illinois*

George: The nest in your photograph is that of a Baltimore oriole. Some consider the female oriole the premier nest weaver among all American birds. She alone uses her sharp black bill to thread grasses, plant fibers, hair, yarn, string, wool and cottony material into a bag or pouch with the opening at the top.

When the young hatch, both parents feed their offspring by standing on the top of the nest and stretching their necks down to the hungry open mouths. These nests are so well-constructed that they often last through the following winter, long after the birds have migrated south.

Serious About Sodium

Are salted nuts OK to feed to birds? I know birds need some salt, but is this too much?

RHIANNON THUNELL, *Greenwood, Indiana*

George: Yes, salted nuts are fine. If birds have been eating too much salt, they'll take a pass on salty snacks. We often don't give our avian friends enough credit for knowing what their bodies need and what to avoid.

Identity Crisis ▶

I saw this bird in my yard in late September. Can you tell me what it is?

JOHN STURDIVANT
Jonesville, North Carolina

George: Strange as it may seem, your bird is a male scarlet tanager. Where is the scarlet, you may ask. Each autumn, as migration time approaches in the North, male scarlet tanagers molt their red feathers and grow yellow ones. They retain their black wings, but they are otherwise yellow until the spring breeding season is near.

▲ Bill Mishap?

I spotted the above thrasher with a very elongated and oddly shaped bill. What could have happened to it?

LYNN DRAUS, *Cary, North Carolina*

George: Deformed bills in birds are quite rare. Research into the subject shows that some bird families are more prone to bill deformities than others. The mimic thrush family, which includes the brown thrasher pictured here, is among those where deformed bills are more common.

For example, six brown thrashers with sickle-shaped bills were reported in Florida in the 1960s. Scientists don't fully understand these abnormalities, but they suggest that injury, genetics and chemical pollution are the likely causes.

Non-Bathers

I keep feeders, birdhouses and baths available in my yard year-round. I have noticed that when it is cool in early spring and late fall, the birds plop right into the bath to drink and bathe. However, when our weather turns warm in the summer, they drink but never bathe. Can you explain this behavior?

KRISTI BITLER, *Derby, Kansas*

George: I find that my birdbath is used all summer, especially in hot weather. If your birdbath is in the sun, the water may be too hot for the birds. Try placing your bath in the shade and maybe that will lure the birds into the water to cool themselves and clean their feathers.

Puzzling Little Birds ▶

Every year in northern Mississippi, several pairs of these diminutive birds appear at our feeder. My best guess is that they're prairie warblers, but I'm not sure. Can you tell me what they are?

JOHN PFISTER, *Batesville, Mississippi*

George: Warblers migrating through your state in the fall are hard to identify because they're not dressed in breeding plumage. I believe that we're looking at pine warblers, but of different genders: The top one is a male and the bottom, a female. They're also among the few warblers that stop at feeders.

Welcome Winter Visitors

It's not common to see red-headed woodpeckers in my area. However, last winter I had two pairs in our trees and at the suet feeder. But now they've disappeared. How can I attract them again?

LAURIE LACROIX, *Yankton, South Dakota*

George: Red-headed woodpeckers usually are summer residents of your state, meaning they come there to nest. Then they often spend winters south of you in the south-central plains and the Southeast.

First, make sure what you saw were red-headed woodpeckers. Red-bellied woodpeckers also have red heads and spend the winter in your area, so perhaps that was it. Either way, the best winter food for woodpeckers is suet, either from the meat department or blocks you can buy at the store. Keep suet feeders filled, and perhaps you'll attract woodpeckers this winter as well.

Picking Flowers

Several birds are pulling the blossoms off our flowering crab tree. They pull

them off, hold them in their mouths for a few seconds and then drop them. Why are they doing this?

JO ANNE ERDMANN, *Manistee, Michigan*

George: It sounds as if these birds are after the nectar in the center of the bloom. So once they remove the nectar or edible center of the flower, they drop the petals to the ground. It's a good reminder that flowering trees provide much more than just pretty spring blossoms.

▼ Out on a Wire

While on a nature walk, I saw these birds sitting high on a wire. I cannot identify them. What are they?

KAREN SALYER, *Belmont, Michigan*

George: The two birds on the wire are barn swallows. Their forked tails and coloring distinguish them from other swallows. As the species name suggests, they prefer to nest under the eaves of barns.

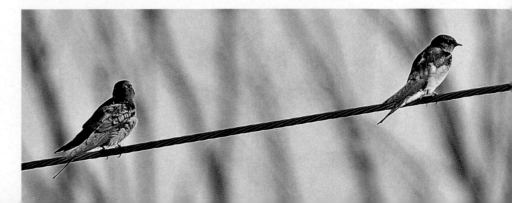

Baltimore oriole
Photo by Richard Day / Daybreak Imagery

Blue-winged warbler
Photo by Bill Leaman

White-breasted nuthatch
Photo by Carol L. Edwards

Northern cardinal
Photo by Tony Campbell /
Shutterstock.com

Eastern bluebirds
Grand prize winner in our Backyard Photo Contest
Photo by Michelle Holland

CHAPTER 2

Hummingbird
heaven

Discover the traits that make hummingbirds so special. Find budget-friendly ways to attract flying jewels to your yard. Learn trusted tricks for capturing these intriguing little fliers on camera.

RUFOUS HUMMINGBIRD; ROLF NUSSBAUMER

A FRIENDLY WELCOME.
A female ruby-throat hovers at petunias, looking for a sweet treat.

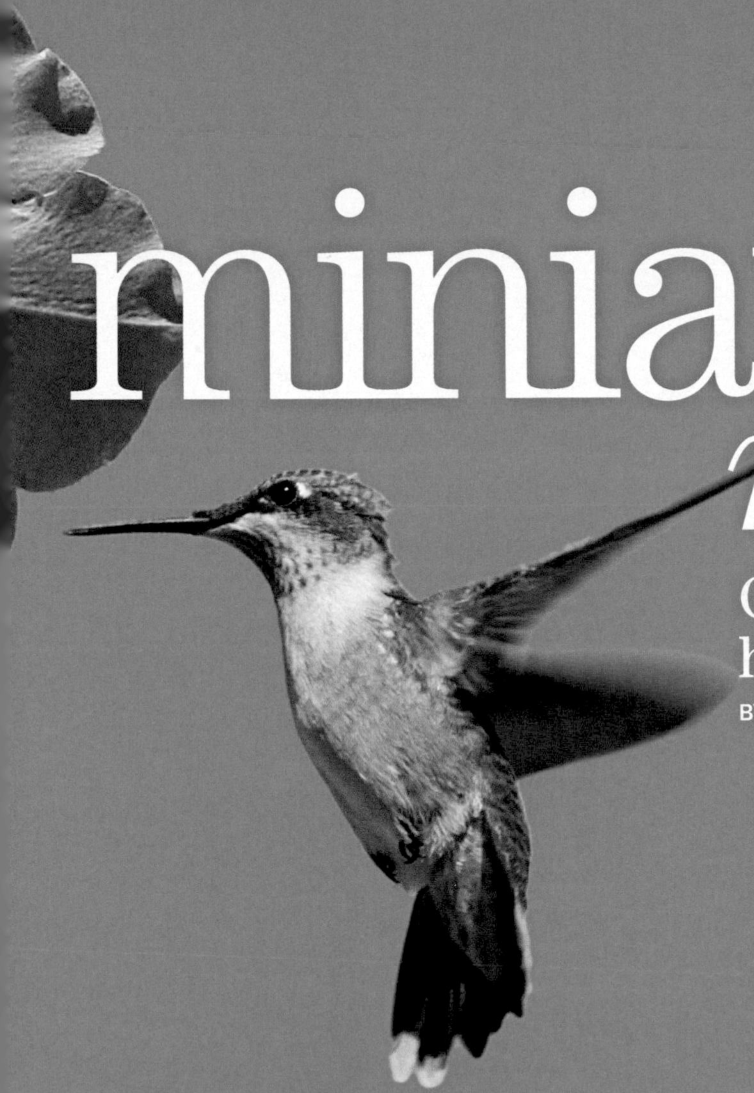

miniature
marvels

Celebrate the high-energy hustle of hummingbirds.

BY KENN AND KIMBERLY KAUFMAN

Hummingbirds seem to exist in a different dimension from other birds. If we look around, we can see basic similarities in the lives of sparrows, crows, quail, woodpeckers and just about every other kind of bird. But hummingbirds are different.

They appear to be living in a separate, whimsical world. And the fact that we can witness the magic show in our own gardens—or even right outside our windows—makes hummingbirds all the more endearing.

Endless Energy

Hummingbirds' miniature dimensions make them all the more amazing. A ruby-throat or rufous weighs about one-ninth of an ounce. That's lighter than a nickel!

The sight of a hummer darting about the garden is even more impressive when we break this high-speed action down by the numbers. A hummingbird at rest may breathe four times per second, and its heart may beat more than 20 times per second.

A hummingbird may also beat its wings 80 times a second. To get a sense of what this means, stand up and flap your arms as fast as you can for a few moments. If you concentrate, you should be able to flap four times in a second. Now imagine doing this 20 times faster—an impossible feat for a human, but nothing remarkable for a hummingbird.

At first glance, hummingbirds often seem delightfully tame, even confiding. Sometimes they'll come astonishingly close, especially if you're near a feeder or a natural nectar source.

Think about it from their perspective, though. Human beings must seem like incredibly big, slow creatures to them. They're likely to be more interested in things closer to their own size and speed.

Spiders, for instance, may make you squeamish, but if you love hummingbirds, you have to appreciate spiders. Hummingbirds often use bits of spiderweb for their nests. Strong, lightweight and super sticky, it's the perfect nest material, allowing for compact nests that will stretch as the baby hummers begin to mature.

Protecting Their Turf

An endless sugar rush fuels the high-speed comings and goings of these miniature marvels. Many birds feed on nectar, but none do it as consistently as hummingbirds.

STAY OUT OF THE WAY. Male hummingbirds are often territorial around feeding zones. Above is a male ruby-throat and at lower right is a Lucifer hummingbird. Both will go to great lengths to defend their turf from other hummingbirds.

And this dependence on flower nectar happens to drive much of their interesting behavior.

Consider their defense of territory. A pair of robins will guard a space of an acre or so during the nesting season, driving away all other robins. This territory will supply food, water and shelter for the pair of robins and their offspring. After the nesting season, though, robins gather in flocks and stop defending their space.

Hummingbirds, in contrast, may defend a temporary feeding territory at any time of year. Flowers produce only so much nectar in a day, so if a hummer finds a good patch of blooms, it may start defending that patch, driving away all other hummers.

All the zooming and chattering of hummingbirds chasing away rivals may seem like a waste of energy to us, but it may be easier than flying off and finding another flower patch. It becomes somewhat comical, though, when the instinct carries over to hummingbirds visiting feeders. The feeders may have a vast supply of sugar water, but the birds don't see it that way. The instinct to guard their food source is so strong that the hummer wars may continue all day.

PUT UP A FIGHT.
Hummingbird battles over
territory consist mostly of
posturing and bill-pointing,
as these two are doing.

hummingbird heaven   47

IN CONSTANT MOTION. This broad-billed hummingbird (above, left) and female black-chinned hummingbird are always on the move, especially when nectar-filled blooms are nearby. High-speed photography might make the birds seem motionless in midair, but their wings are actually beating dozens of times every second. At near left, a rufous hummingbird is perched, and two nestling Anna's hummingbirds get ready to fledge (far left).

The reliance on flowers also drives their migration patterns. In the West, for example, species like the rufous, broad-tailed and calliope hummers migrate north through the deserts and valleys in very early spring and south through the mountain meadows in late summer. Why? Because that's where the flowers are. In early spring, mountain meadows are still covered with snow, while in late summer the valleys may be hot and dry, so the hummers have adapted their routes to follow the blooming seasons.

Energy Drink

One summer, when we discovered a female ruby-throat building a nest in our Ohio backyard, we witnessed an example of just how extraordinary a hummingbird's energy can be.

Just an hour after finding the first nest, we discovered another one in the front yard, with two large young almost ready to fly. Because Kimberly had searched for years without finding one of these well-camouflaged nests, we were stunned at the coincidence of finding two on the same day.

But the real surprise came a few hours later, when we realized that the same female hummer was tending both nests!

Our little overachiever was building a second nest even while she was still feeding two demanding, nearly full-grown nestlings in the

first one. And since the male does absolutely nothing to assist with the nest or the young (as Kimberly often points out to Kenn), this female ruby-throat was doing everything on her own. Her sheer hustle was nothing short of astounding!

That two bird "experts" can still learn something new about a species as common as a ruby-throat is a powerful reminder that no matter how much we think we know, there are still endless discoveries to be made. And we need look no farther than our own backyards to be amazed, impressed, astonished and blessed by even the tiniest of birds.

hummer happenings

Your "bird tales" celebrate all things hummingbird.

Giving Mom a Hand

A juvenile hummingbird flew into our open garage but couldn't find its way out. When I entered the garage, it flew across to me and landed at my feet. Gently, I picked it up and took it outside, placing it on the hummingbird feeder. Almost immediately, its mother flew in and perched protectively behind her young. Luckily, I had my camera with me and captured this amazing moment just before they both flew away.

MARILYN OSBORNE
Youngsville, North Carolina

Plucky Customers ▼

A novice bird-watcher and photographer, I walked for miles through the Rattlesnake Wilderness area near my home trying to catch up to any pretty bird for a snapshot. But when I kept scaring the birds away, I soon decided that picking an area with lots of activity for a bird blind would improve my luck. Almost immediately, a male calliope showed up, dive-bombing me to investigate.

On my next visit, I filled a red bottle cap with sugar water and set it on a nearby branch. In minutes, several hummers—some calliopes and a rufous—came to feed. After drinking themselves silly, they perched just feet from me, maybe to get a good look at their waitress!

JOAN ZEIBER
Missoula, Montana

One of Joan's calliope friends

Hurricane Hummer

With everyone anxiously preparing for Hurricane Irene last year, I joked that I'd better make sure I filled the hummingbird feeder.

As green leaves shook off trees and rain came in sheets, we spied something on the nectar feeder. Using binoculars, we were shocked to see a single hummingbird out, enduring that raging storm. It would drink, then sit back to brace itself against the punishing winds. Our little friend stayed half an hour, then left briefly, but came back for another go at its favorite feeder.

We couldn't believe it. Our emergency hummingbird plans were no joke at all!

KATHLEEN MOCKO, *Little Falls, New York*

hummer happenings

You're in My Seat

Our hummingbirds often perch in a large cypress near the front porch. Our free-range pet chickens also perch in trees, roosting in low branches every night to stay safe from predators.

One evening, my favorite hen had injured her leg, so I helped her roost by tucking her into the branches of the nearby cypress. Minutes later, a dozen or so hummingbirds flew rapid circles around her, some aggressively darting inside the branches and charging my hen, who simply ignored them. How amazing to see these normally competitive birds working together to defend their tree.

CHIP KIRKPATRICK, *Yulee, Florida*

▼ Holy Hummer Haven!

Our hummingbird hobby is getting a little out of hand! We hang an average of 40 feeders around our porch each summer and have gone through as much as 280 pounds of sugar in a single season. Since this photo was taken, we've added benches to the deck and are growing flowers and vines all along the rails. It's a handful to maintain, but we never need to travel for a vacation, because our porch is a hummingbird paradise.

BOB & BARB BADGER, *Buchanan, Tennessee*

White Wonder

On a recent evening, a fellow birder friend observed what he thought was a white moth feeding on spotted touch-me-not flowers (also known as jewelweed). Upon closer inspection, he realized it was a leucistic immature female ruby-throated hummingbird.

Fortunately, she stayed around for several days, affording me many photo opportunities. Our pale friend fed repeatedly on the spotted touch-me-nots, which often attract premigratory hummingbirds because of the nectar's high energy content. Although challenging, capturing images of this rare bird was most rewarding!

LEW SCHARPF, *Auburn, Alabama*

Feed Me Now

Last summer I had just one hummingbird, which liked to perch on my clothesline. One day it kept flying from the clothesline to me, back to the clothesline, back to me, until I finally noticed its feeder was empty. I filled it, and as I went back to hang it up, the tiny bird came buzzing around me. I slowly held the feeder out at arm's length, and the hummer flew right up and drank from it again and again!

EVELYN KRAUTKRAMER
Saukville, Wisconsin

Neighborly to Nesters ▶

In a past issue of *Birds & Blooms*, I read a suggestion that said putting scraps of yarn and string in a suet cage provides handy nesting material for visiting birds. I stuffed a feeder full, hung it outside my window and waited anxiously.

Here's just one shot of the wee hummingbirds that came and went, snatching up the fuzzy bits. It didn't take many days before the feeder was empty. My birds and I thank you for the handy tip!

JUNE THOMPSON
Deer Harbor, Washington

▼ Bumbling Into Trouble

I was stunned to look at my feeder through the kitchen window and see a male ruby-throat with a bee impaled on his bill! The bee's wings and legs moved, and the hummer was frantic, trying to scrape the bee off using the perch or kick it off with his foot.

The hummingbird was too panicky for me to help. I watched it leave the feeder, return, fly up in the air, shake its head and have a miserable time. At least it could still feed. Hours later, the bird exhausted, I slowly lifted the window, reached out and grasped it gently. I pulled at the bee just a little, and the terrified hummer gave a muffled cry. I tried again, this time with tweezers, and carefully pulled off the bee. I opened my hand and the hummingbird was gone!

I kept watching for him, hoping he was OK. At dusk, he stopped by. What a relief! That was one anxious day, and I hope my feathered friend now stays far away from bumblebees.

MICHELLE TRENT, *Shelby, North Carolina*

a bee caught on its bill!

My Hummingbird Summer

Nearly two years ago, I spotted a hummingbird nest in my backyard: small, well-camouflaged and built almost 12 feet up in the branches of our ash tree. The mother had made it from moss, lichen, spiderwebs and fluff from trees and plants, and I watched it stretch as her young grew.

After 16 days, one of the two tiny eggs hatched, and in 22 days more, the juvenile fledged from the nest. After that, I'd stand for hours, holding a red cap of nectar in my left palm, camera in my right hand, waiting patiently. Almost two weeks later, the mother hummingbird finally landed in my hand. It was an amazing summer experience I'll always treasure.

LOLA PRYOR, *Caledonia, Ohio*

1

bloomers for hummingbirds

These long-blooming flowers will keep hummingbirds fed for months!

When we started working on this year's hummingbird issue, we knew our Top 10 would be a challenge. We've done general stories in the past about hummingbirds' favorite plants, so we wanted something extra special.

Then we thought, *Wouldn't everyone want to know which hummingbird plants have especially long bloom times?* With these tiny fliers showing up in spring and hanging around through late summer or early fall, it would be good to know what you can really count on for months at a time.

So we checked with our gardening genius, Melinda Myers, and came up with this list. The floral favorites here should help you entice more hummingbirds than ever!

1 Columbine

(Aquilegia, Zones 3 to 9)
This native wildlife magnet has striking blossoms that hummingbirds can't resist. It grows up to 3 feet high and blooms in many different colors. Need another reason to consider columbine? It's low-maintenance, too.
WHY WE LOVE IT: Most blooms are a mix of shades, like white and red or white and purple, making a bold statement in the garden.

2 Phlox

(Phlox, Zones 3 to 9)
Butterflies crave it, hummingbirds can't resist it, it smells delicious, the flowers are gorgeous—the list goes on and on. For upright phlox cultivars (garden phlox), choose disease-resistant Tiara or David. For a more sprawling ground cover and early blooms, try creeping phlox.
WHY WE LOVE IT: A little bit of phlox goes a long way. It multiplies quickly, so you can divide and conquer other parts of your yard with this resilient bloomer.

5 Salvia

(Salvia, Zones 4 to 10)
You'll see a plethora of red salvia flats at the garden center in spring. These are annuals, and they're popular with hummers. But pick up a few salvias in the perennial department, too. The trumpet-shaped flowers come in blue, red, orange, white, pink and purple. Grow in full sun or light shade and they'll bloom for months.
WHY WE LOVE IT: The Black and Blue Gargantica cultivar (pictured here) has gorgeous deep-blue blooms that last.

6 Pineapple sage

(Salvia elegans, annual)
An annual in the salvia family, this sage is fairly new to the market. Proven Winners introduced this cultivar, Golden Delicious, which boasts lovely yellow foliage and bright-red blooms. It does very well in the heat, and it's a champ in containers.
WHY WE LOVE IT: The leaves really are pineapple-scented, so you'll like them as much as the hummers do.

9 Cigar flower

(Cuphea ignea, Zones 10 to 11)
This plant is one of the gardening world's best-kept secrets, with long tubular blooms that shine from spring through autumn. Unless you're in Zone 10 or 11, think of it as an annual. Once you see the results you get, it'll become a staple in your garden every year.
WHY WE LOVE IT: It's a natural for hanging baskets. You can mingle it with other plants, but it's a star on its own, too.

10 Lungwort

(Pulmonaria, Zones 2 to 8)
Don't let the funky name keep you from adding it to your backyard. You can always count on lungwort, which emerges in early spring in shades of blue, pink, white or purple. Those pretty spring blooms are a good source of early nectar and the foliage lasts all season.
WHY WE LOVE IT: It's often grown for its foliage, so you get a plant with multiple attractions!

3

Bee balm

(*Monarda*, Zones 3 to 9)

This flower is a staple in any hummingbird garden, and it has a fun shape to boot! Find it in its traditional red or in newer shades of purple, pink and white. It's also a native; another reason to give it a try.

WHY WE LOVE IT: It reseeds readily and smells great when you're weeding out excess plants in spring. Plus, it's easy to grow, especially if you choose mildew-resistant options like Marshall's Delight or Jacob Cline.

4

Fuchsia

(*Fuchsia*, annual)

One of the most recognizable annuals around, fuchsia has dainty flowers that resemble ballerinas. Hummingbirds flock to the red, purple, white and pink blooms. You can find both dwarf and upright varieties, but most grow from 6 to 24 inches. With more options on the market than ever before, it's time to plant this charmer.

WHY WE LOVE IT: It's made for the shade! If you want to hang a basket under an eave, fuchsia will thrive in it.

7

Verbena

(*Verbena* x *hybrida*, annual)

You'll find dozens of new verbenas on the market, including the popular Superbena line by Proven Winners, but the red verbena pictured here is the Aztec Dark Red cultivar from Ball Horticultural Co. Grow in a container or in an annual bed for endless summer blooms.

WHY WE LOVE IT: The color options are infinite, so it's easy to find one that will work for you.

8

Cardinal flower

(*Lobelia cardinalis*, Zones 3 to 9)

You can choose a sunny or partly shady spot with moist soil for this bold red flower. It grows up to 4 feet tall and has plenty of blooms to go around for all your hummingbird visitors. Plant it this year. You won't regret it.

WHY WE LOVE IT: It's an age-old favorite that never seems to fail to attract hummers. Plus, we love that "cardinal" is in the name.

the power of purple

Sure, red flowers are hummingbird naturals, but they're not the only ones our beloved flying jewels adore. The sweet scents of the purple blooms in this container are sure to entice. Plant this combination in full sun in an 18-inch pot.

A Angelface® Blue summer snapdragon (1)
B Superbells® Dreamsicle calibrachoa (3)
C Supertunia® Bordeaux petunia (2)
D ColorBlaze® LifeLime coleus (1)

birds IN WINTER

You may catch a glimpse of these gorgeous fliers when the temperature dips. Here's why.

BY KENN KAUFMAN

Could any birds say summer more clearly than hummingbirds? Dancing before flowers to sip nectar, flashing and glittering in the light, they seem like tiny sunbeams come to life.

The very idea of winter hummingbirds sounds almost like a contradiction. But some hummingbirds do spend the winter in North America, and in recent years their numbers and range have been increasing.

Year-Round With Anna

Of course, winter isn't a harsh season everywhere. In coastal California, where the weather is moderate year-round, Anna's hummingbirds have always been permanent residents.

Historically, they were common from Baja north to the San Francisco Bay region. Around the 1930s, however, they began to spread. By the 1960s they were expanding eastward and beginning to nest in Arizona. At the same time, they pushed north through coastal Oregon and Washington and into southwestern British Columbia.

Today you can see male Anna's flashing their rose-red crowns and singing their scratchy songs in Vancouver, even on cold days in January.

What made it possible for these hummingbirds to expand their range so dramatically? The short answer is that gardeners did.

With well-watered parks and yards boasting hardy plants blooming in every season, we created a landscape that would support more Anna's hummingbirds year-round than most of their natural habitats. Add in a generous number of sugar-water feeders, and you have a hummer haven for all seasons.

Taking a Detour

A similar story has played out in the eastern states. But the plot line there is more complicated and involves different players.

Most varieties of hummingbirds in the U.S. live in the West, especially the Southwest. Originally, the only hummers east of the Great Plains were the familiar little ruby-throats. They were summer birds from the Gulf

 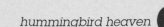

Coast to southern Canada, but almost all went to southern Mexico or Central America for the winter, with only a handful remaining in Florida.

But recent decades have seen a virtual explosion in the numbers of western hummingbirds wandering eastward. Leading the charge has been the rufous hummingbird.

This copper-colored sprite is among the most numerous western hummers, spending early summer in Northwestern forests, from Oregon and Montana to the edge of Alaska. In late summer and early fall, most of the population migrates south through mountain meadows of the Rockies, heading for a wintering range in Mexico. But every fall, a few rufous hummingbirds stray east out of the Rockies, winding up in the southeastern U.S.

In centuries past, such strays probably would not have survived the winter—not unless they corrected their course and headed for Mexico.

There simply weren't enough wildflowers to sustain them through the season. However, gardeners have changed that equation, too.

Over the last century, legions of plant lovers throughout the South have developed year-round flower beds. In the process, they have unwittingly changed the landscape to support winter hummingbirds.

Growing Numbers

Rufous hummingbirds now spend the winter in Louisiana, Mississippi, Alabama, Georgia and Florida, with smaller numbers north along the Atlantic Coast to Virginia and beyond. And these birds seem to have brought their friends along.

The calliope hummingbird, America's tiniest bird at just over 3 inches, is now a regular in winter in the Southeastern states. So is the broad-tailed, another bird from the Rockies, and the black-chinned hummingbird, the western counterpart to the ruby-throat. During recent seasons, 10 or more different species of hummers have spent the winter in the Gulf states.

Creating a Haven

Many people in the South now work at developing winter hummingbird

Ruby-throated hummingbird

gardens, putting up sugar-water feeders and planting any kind of red, tubular flower that will bloom when the weather is cool.

Knowing that hummers will pause to investigate anything in their favorite color, one Louisiana birder even painted her house red! Any hummingbird that flew within a mile of that place probably detoured to check it out.

Most people wouldn't go as far as that Louisiana woman. But if you live in a climate where it's possible to keep some flowers blooming during the winter, why not try planting some hardy nectar sources for hummers? You just might make the joyful discovery that hummingbirds can be winter birds after all.

WINTER SIGHTINGS. If you live in the Midwest or Northeast, your best bet is to travel. If you already have a vacation planned this winter to somewhere sunny, do a little research ahead of time to see if hummingbirds are in that specific area. Then take a little detour to check them out!

Calliope hummingbird

Anna's hummingbird

for less

Lure hummingbirds to your yard with these frugal hints.

money-saving hummingbird secrets

Female rufous hummingbird at scarlet gilia flower

Make a Hummingbird Perch!

We all know hummingbirds are territorial and a little aggressive near feeders. So give them a place to keep watch and wait their turn for the feeder. Mike Eastman of Henderson, Nevada, makes these hummingbird perches and hangs them near his feeders and in his flower garden. Make your own with these simple steps:

- Use wood glue to attach dowels to the main post.
- Decorate with paint—a good art project for kids. And, of course, think red!
- If you're hanging the perch, you should probably put some weight on the bottom of the main post to help stabilize it in the wind. Anything weighing more than 4 ounces will do.

GIVE 'EM A SPECIAL TREAT. Overripe cantaloupe? Put it out for the hummingbirds. They'll devour it instead of it going to waste.

GO RED! While flowers are ideal, just about anything that's red will interest hummingbirds. Attach leftover ribbons, bows, pieces of an old scarf or even artificial flowers to your feeder and see them buzz in.

MAKE YOUR SUGAR WATER, don't buy it. Remember, all it takes is 4 parts water to 1 part sugar. Boil it, cool it, and voilà! No need for store-bought nectar. Skip the red food coloring, too. It's not necessary.

BE PATIENT AND RELAX. It doesn't cost anything to take a seat in your backyard and enjoy the sights and sounds—and, if you're lucky, hummingbirds!

CHOOSE WISELY. If you set up your hummer feeders in the shade, there's less opportunity for algae and some types of bacteria to grow, so you won't have to change the sugar water nearly as often.

DOUBLE UP. Save time and money by giving your old toothbrush a new life: Use it to scrub those hard-to-reach parts of a sugar-water feeder, inside and out.

ATTRACT NESTERS. Go ahead and let your dandelions go to seed. The hummingbirds will use the seeds to line their nests.

DON'T GET FANCY. Anything that holds water can be made into a feeder. If it's red, so much the better. So make your own, or just stick with inexpensive, basic feeders. The hummers won't care.

REMEMBER YOUR SUCCESSES. If you've had a lot of luck luring hummers with cannas or bee balm, stick with them. Don't bother wasting money on different plants that may not work as well.

take amazing hummingbird
PHOTOS

Use these tips from readers like you.

Get to know your camera.
Play with the settings before the hummingbirds arrive. I know which settings will give me my sharpest image (an ISO of 800 with an f-stop of 8). I also like to use a flash. Sometimes hummingbirds aren't in direct sun, so using a flash might help bring out their beautiful iridescence.

◀ **Broad-billed hummingbird**
BY JAMES ORRIS
Phoenix, Arizona

Use a tripod.
Set it up about 15 feet from a flower that a hummer is likely to visit. Position yourself so you'll be able to get a profile shot of the bird while it's hovering at the blossom. If your camera has a bracketing feature, use it. It will take multiple photos with one click of the shutter to give you your best shot.

◀ **Black-chinned hummingbird**
BY LARRY WILSON, *Austin, Texas*

Use movable flower boxes to your advantage.
I have two that I can move to maximize stopping points and get different backgrounds. I also try to have the sun at my back; both sunrise and sunset are ideal times. And I make sure to position myself and my flowers so that my view is clear. Finally, I make note of the flowers and the spots the hummingbirds visit most often so I'll know where they'll be before they get there.

◀ **Ruby-throated hummingbird**
BY LARRY KELLER, *Lititz, Pennsylvania*

Use water to your advantage.

I look forward to spring and summer, when I can put solar fountains in my birdbaths. The Anna's and rufous hummingbirds head for the 6-inch-high water spray as soon as the sun comes up. I grab my camera and stand not too far from the bath, making sure there's a fairly solid background behind my photo. The small bamboo fence I added to disguise my chain-link fence makes for better pictures!

Anna's hummingbird ▶
BY VICKI MILLER
Kelseyville, California

Patience, patience!

It's easy to hang around my feeder and photograph the hummer traffic, but to me that feels like cheating. I prefer finding a garden that is filled with colorful flowers and has a nice flat rock to sit on. Most hummingbirds are shy, so I try to go on my own whenever possible. And keep this in mind: Put the birds' safety, health and happiness ahead of the photos. That way you can feel good about sharing their space.

Broad-tailed hummingbird ▶
BY CONNIE BLUE
Oklahoma City, Oklahoma

Observe from a distance.

Hummingbirds take pains to protect their food. They'll often find a perch that gives them a view of the food source and any potential intruders. So locate that protective perch and photograph them there. Also, find a well-protected spot for yourself: Hide behind a post, a hanging plant or even a tree trunk. Keep in mind that natural settings are best, so spend some time among the flowers, too.

Rufous hummingbird ▶
BY RON NEWHOUSE, *Bryan, Texas*

61

hummingbird
glad you asked!

Backyard Bird-Watcher George Harrison is here to answer your toughest questions!

To Boil or Not to Boil?

Should I boil sugar water for hummingbirds? What is the benefit?

TOM MISKA, *Minneapolis, Minnesota*

George: It makes no difference to the birds if you boil the water, but boiling does make it mix faster with the sugar. Or if you don't have the purest water in your area, boiling is a good idea. Mix 4 parts water to 1 part sugar. No coloring is necessary.

Hummingbird Development

When do the bills of hummingbirds develop? How do they peck themselves out of the egg?

MABEL NISLEY, *Middlebury, Indiana*

George: The bills of baby hummingbirds still in the shell are soft and short. Like all other birds, they have an "egg tooth" on the top of the bill that is used to cut the shell; they lose this tooth after they hatch. The bills grow in strength, but they don't reach their full length until after a bird leaves the nest.

Courting or Combat?

Near the hummingbird feeder in my backyard, I saw two hummingbirds close together, face to face. They lowered themselves almost to the ground, then went straight up into the tree, facing each other all the while. Was this a mating ritual or were they facing off in combat?

CONNIE KASAL, *Belle Plaine, Iowa*

Overgrown Hummingbird

In early June, this large hummingbird visited my feeder for about three days. I could hear it coming because of its loud chirps. It was almost too big to drink out of the feeder holes. Can you tell me more about it?

JEANNE WIMBERLEY
Pie Town, New Mexico

George: The two largest hummingbirds in North America are the blue-throated and the magnificent, both of which can be found in the southwestern part of your state. I don't know which species this is, but my guess is the magnificent because of the heavily spotted breast.

George: If the two hummingbirds were of opposite gender, it was a mating ritual. But if they were the same gender, it was a challenge for territory or a food source.

Because you saw this in Iowa, the hummers were probably ruby-throated, the primary hummingbird species that breeds east of the Rockies. Males and females are very different in appearance. The male has the ruby-red throat; the female is green on the back and white below. A male hummingbird performs an impressive courtship display flight above the female, which is usually perched in a tree.

Anna's at the Ash Pile

I always see Anna's hummingbirds licking our wood ash discard pile. Do you know why they do this? What are they after?

JANINE GIANINO, *Menlo Park, California*

George: I've never heard of a hummingbird, or any bird for that matter, being attracted to wood ash. They may be trying to get rid of parasites by rubbing the ash into their feathers, or they could be using it to build nests. It's less likely that they're eating it, though it's possible the ash contains some mineral that they crave.

Disappearing Act

I live in the northwest corner of Arkansas. Every spring the hummingbirds are here for a month and then disappear. In June, they come back to the feeders. Why do they leave, and where do they go?

NORENE BARNES
Siloam Springs, Arkansas

George: The hummingbirds that visit you are migrating. They do not nest in your area. In the springtime, they stop at your feeders en route to their breeding grounds, which are located farther north. Then, in midsummer, they are already headed southward to the tropics for winter, but they take their time and enjoy your handouts.

Living in Harmony

I have an oriole feeder in my backyard, but I've found orioles feeding from the hummingbird feeder in my front yard. Ever since the orioles started feeding in the area, the hummingbirds have not returned. Are the bigger birds scaring the smaller ones away?

PEGGY HASKIN, *Racine, Wisconsin*

George: These birds do share each other's sugar water. But if you want them to stay apart, try putting up at least one of each kind of feeder in each area. Doing so should help separate them.

▲ Hummingbird Antics

For several days, we noticed that about eight Anna's hummingbirds swarmed around one feeder at the same time each evening. What can you tell us about this behavior?

WILLIAM HERRMANNSFELDT
Los Altos, California

George: Waning daylight is probably why so many hummingbirds flock to a feeder at the same time each evening. Hummingbirds tend to feed more just before dark so they have enough energy to survive the night. With the sun setting at about the same time every day, you may notice other birds stocking up then, as well.

▲ Almost Albino

We thought this hummingbird was albino at first, but when we uploaded the pictures, we could see some light brown and tan markings. Any ideas about what it could be?

RON & ROSE SMITH
Ethel, Louisiana

George: This hummingbird has a pigment problem. In other words, it is partially albino, though not a pure albino. Louisiana is known to host wandering western hummingbirds, but the most common and only regular breeding hummingbird in that area is the ruby-throated. This bird is most likely a partial albino ruby-throat.

FAQ

❝ When should I stop feeding hummingbirds in the fall? ❞

George: Because there are other hummingbirds that have spent the nesting season north of your backyard, you'll want to maintain your sugar-water feeders long after the local hummers have departed for the tropics.

Migrating hummingbirds will often stop to recharge at your feeders as they pass through your area. I would stop feeding no sooner than two weeks after you see the last hummer. But even a bit longer can be a good idea. You never know when you'll get a straggler.

build a
hummingbird mister

they love flying through mist!

Better than a birdbath, this easy-to-make water feature is irresistible to hummingbirds.

BY KRIS DRAKE

Hummingbirds love water, but traditional birdbaths often don't do the trick for them. As some of the zippiest birds around, they don't stop all that often just to sit at a bath.

So try an alternative: Give them some mist instead. You can find everything you need at a hardware store or online. A mister adds charm to your yard while attracting some of your favorite birds!

STEP 1. Cut the unthreaded PVC pipe with a pipe cutter or a handsaw. You'll need a 14-in. piece for the left leg and a 15-in. piece for the top.

STEP 2. In the 15-in. piece, drill one hole in the center of the piping for the top mister and two holes for the bottom misters a few inches away. The size of the sprayers will determine the size of the holes you need to drill. See the photo at right for a close look at how the misters fit into the pipe.

STEP 3. Cut 6 in. off one end of the 18-in. piece of PVC; the remainder will be used for the right leg. Without gluing (just to get an idea of the fit), attach the coupling to the end of the threaded pipe and then to the pump. Next, attach the cap to the right leg and the elbows to the top. Stand the "U" shape of PVC upright. Make needed adjustments so the height is equal on both sides.

STEP 4. Remove the coupling and pump and disassemble all of the piping pieces. To help the pieces adhere to one another, rub the ends of the PVC pipe and the insides of the elbows and cap with steel wool. Dust off the pieces. Apply PVC adhesive to the outside of the pipe and connect the elbows and cap. Be sure the holes you drilled for your misters are facing in the correct direction. Let the adhesive dry.

supplies

- 1 unthreaded 1/2-in. PVC pipe, 30 in. long
- 3 EZ-Clone 360 misters
- 1 threaded 1/2-in. PVC pipe, 18 in. long
- One 3/8-in. flare x 1/2-in. FIP coupling
- Submersible pump
- 1 PVC cap for 1/2-in. pipe
- 2 PVC elbows for 1/2-in. pipe
- Steel wool
- PVC cement
- 5-gallon plastic container, about 20 x 16 x 12 in.
- Small rocks or bricks
- Spray primer, paint and finishing spray
- Acrylic paint for decoration

The pump we used is an EcoPlus Eco-100 Submersible Pump. If you're looking for something similar, make sure you use a pump that transfers roughly 100 gallons of water per hour. This will ensure a good mist (as seen above).

STEP 5. Prep your piping and container for painting; lightly sand the piping with steel wool to help the paint adhere. Tape and cover the inside of the container up to the water line. Brush off dust; then spray with a coat of primer and let dry.

STEP 6. Once the primer is dry, paint the piping and container with the colors of your choice.

STEP 7. After all the spray paint is dry, it's time to get creative. Paint flowers or another design with acrylic paint. To protect your work from washing off, spray it with a clear matte finishing spray.

STEP 8. Connect the rest of the pieces. To insert the misters into your piping, use a toothpick to add a small amount of PVC cement to the base of a mister and insert each one into the drilled holes in your piping, making sure not to clog any sprayer openings. Allow to dry.

STEP 9. Next, attach the coupling to the threaded end of your piping and then to the pump. If the seal isn't tight, you may need to add thread seal tape. Place the piping inside the container as shown in the photo at left, and secure in place with small rocks or bricks.

STEP 10. Place the mister outside near hummingbirds' favorite feeder or flowers, add water, and plug in your pump. Enjoy the show!

Ruby-throated hummingbird
in Knock Out rose
Photo by Bill Leaman

Ruby-throat and monarch
visiting butterfly bush
Photo by Herb Brietzke

Bathing hummingbird
Photo by Roy Western

Resting hummingbird
*Photo by Sari ONeal /
Shutterstock.com*

Magnificent hummingbird
*Photo by Peter Lilia /
The Image Bank / Getty Images*

CHAPTER 3

Birding DIY

Tap into your crafting talents and invite birds to stop by with fun, family-friendly projects, including bird feeders, birdhouses and birdbaths! Get inspired by other bird lovers' clever creations.

NEST BOX, HEIDI HESS

reduce, reuse and recycle
BIRDHOUSES

Look at these 13 clever reader ideas for turning everyday items into mini cabins, cottages and more!

1. Home Sweet Home...on Wheels Add whimsy by setting a house atop a pair of roller skates. The designer, Terry, likes to think of it as a mobile home for birds!

BY TERRY MOORE, *Quincy, Illinois*

2. Ready for Takeoff Built from leftover cedar, Jim's tiny plane was spruced up with a little bit of paint and a lot of ingenuity. Now it looks nifty hanging in a carport.

BY JIM CROSSMAN, *North Bend, Washington*

3. Vintage Charm An old wooden Coke crate is the base for this couple's cozy country dwelling. See more designs like this one or buy one for yourself at *piecesofpastimes.etsy.com*.

BY JULIE & CHRIS BOGGESS, *Charleston, West Virginia*

4. Gas Power Follow Betsy's lead and fashion an old gas can into a bird cottage. Here, the can's cap, which she removed to make a doorway, lives on as a decorative element up top. See more of her work at *milepost7.etsy.com*.

BY BETSY HAMRE, *Spokane, Washington*

5. Good to the Last Drop Wanda made her birdhouse from a vintage '50s percolator. All it took was a fresh paint job to perk it right up.

BY WANDA KIRK, *Loganville, Georgia*

6. Tasty Topping To brighten the roof of this birdhouse, Robin raided his wife's bottle cap collection. They add just the right touch to the rustic abode.

BY ROBIN ULERY, *Hanford, California*

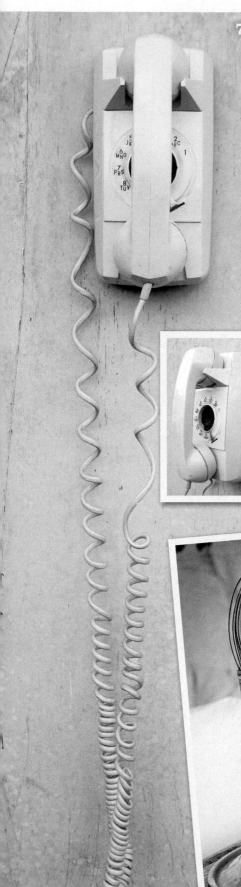

7. Bird Calls This couple found a funky way to recycle old wall phones. Give 'em a ring at *ecocycled.etsy.com*.

BY JEFF & NEECE CAMPIONE, *Fairmont, West Virginia*

8. & 9. Go-Go Gadgets An upcycling pro, Brian made both the copper teapot confection and the bright-blue license plate one. You'll find more of his one-of-a-kind designs at *gadgetsponge.com*.

BY BRIAN CARLISLE, *Shreveport, Louisiana*

10. Into the Woods Growing up, Jeanette adored watching her mom make birdhouses. Now, Jeanette likes to include reclaimed wood in all her designs because she loves knowing that each piece has a story. See more of her work at *sopurdycreations.etsy.com*.

BY JEANETTE PURDY, *Meridian, Idaho*

11. Farm-Fresh Flavor Ted made this birdhouse out of materials from old barns using wood for the body and other finds to dress it up. The top of the house is a flame finial from a vintage lamp. See additional designs at *roundhouseworks.etsy.com*.

BY TED FREEMAN, *Lawrence, Kansas*

12. Mad About Mosaics From corks to gems to glass flowers, you never know what you'll find in the birdhouses by Layla, who's a big fan of mosaic art. Learn more at *winestonebirdhouses.etsy.com*.

BY LAYLA COATS, *Bend, Oregon*

13. Designer Homes Kimberly runs up fashion-forward birdhouses with names like Vera Wing, Ralf Le Wren and Vireo Bradley. Recycled purse straps, belts, drawer handles and household trinkets make for divine designs.

BY KIMBERLY MCRITCHIE, *Port Clinton, Ohio*

10 11

12 13

for less

Whip up some goodies for the birds—on a budget.

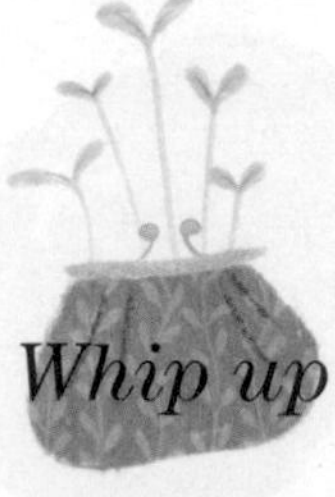

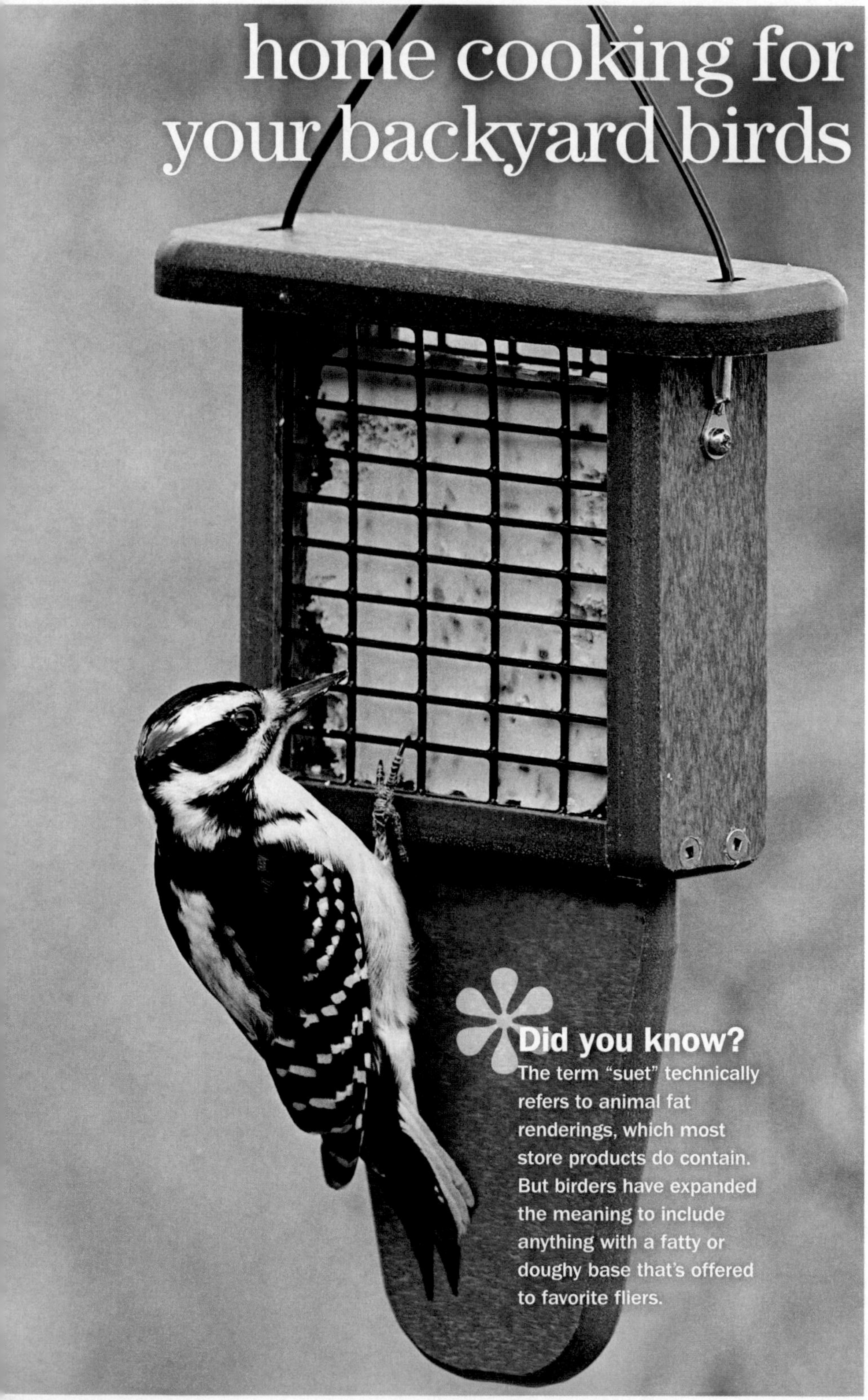

home cooking for your backyard birds

Did you know?
The term "suet" technically refers to animal fat renderings, which most store products do contain. But birders have expanded the meaning to include anything with a fatty or doughy base that's offered to favorite fliers.

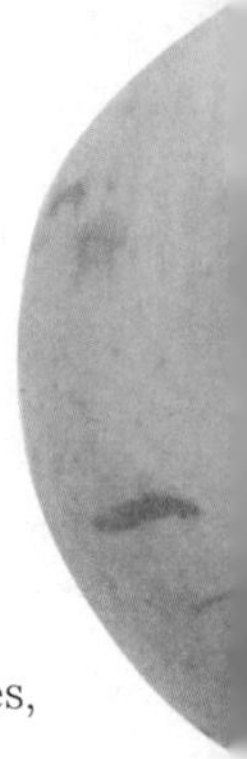

Save money this fall and winter by making your own suet. Our readers share their favorite recipes.

HAMMING IT UP. I had leftover oats and raisins from baking cookies, as well as drippings from a ham. So I melted the ham drippings and some peanut butter together in the microwave. Then I mixed in the oats, raisins and some birdseed. I poured the mixture into a cake pan and froze it. The next day, I cut pieces to fit my suet feeders and put some out for the birds. It was all gone in a day and a half! The jays were especially happy. Best of all, it hardly cost a thing.

SANDRA PARKER, *Glen Burnie, Maryland*

OUT ON A LIMB. I like to spread my suet on tree limbs so more birds can get to it at one time. Here's a recipe I've put together. The birds can't get enough of it, even the juncos.

1 cup cornmeal
1 cup sugar
½ cup flour
¾ cup water
1 cup peanut butter
1 cup lard
1 cup raisins

In a medium bowl, mix the dry ingredients. Then add water, and mix. Put peanut butter and lard in a small bowl and microwave for two minutes. Add to the cornmeal mixture along with the raisins. Refrigerate for about two hours.

NAOMI MANALO, *Middleton, Delaware*

ROUND IT OUT. Pack suet in a ball and offer it on a string. Better yet, put an apple on a second string (a wine cork keeps it in place) to provide fruit at the same time.

THREE-INGREDIENT SUET. This is an easy mixture that keeps my backyard birds very happy.

⅓ loaf stale dry bread
1 can fruit cocktail
½ cup peanut butter

In a food processor, break down the bread, along with the fruit cocktail. Mix with the peanut butter. (You might need a little more or less, depending on how much bread you have.) Place in mesh bags to hang in the trees.

DEB OWEN, *Dowagiac, Michigan*

SUET WITH BENEFITS. I work at a Wild Birds Unlimited store, and I'm always encouraging my customers to create their own recipes filled with fat (rather than less healthful sugars and grains) to best benefit the birds. Here's my simple method for making suet-type food.

2 cups shelled, unsalted peanuts
½ cup raisins
2 to 3 tablespoons cornmeal

Blend peanuts in a food processor until they're the consistency of peanut butter. Then add the raisins and process for another minute. Add the cornmeal and process again. Press this mixture into a mold of your choice. This recipe will have the greatest nutritional value for your feathered friends.

LINDA POPEJOY, *Concord, North Carolina*

OLDIE BUT GOODIE. This recipe is a variation of one I found in an old issue of *Birds & Blooms*. Pygmy nuthatches visit our backyard in the mountains of northern Arizona nearly every day for this.

2 cups crunchy peanut butter
2 cups lard
4 cups oatmeal
4 cups cornmeal
2 cups flour
⅔ cup sugar
1 cup dried fruit
1 cup birdseed

In a microwave, melt the peanut butter and lard in a bowl. Mix together the remaining ingredients and, in a large bowl, slowly combine everything with an electric mixer. When mixture is the consistency of cookie dough, pour into a 9-in. x 13-in. cake pan. With a sharp knife, score the "cake" into about 30 squares. Use a spatula to lift each square onto a sheet of waxed paper. Wrap individually and freeze. When ready to serve, unwrap a frozen cake and place it in a hanging wire suet basket.

PAM DASE, *Pinedale, Arizona*

marvelous mosaics

Readers piece together gorgeous designs for the birds.

Glass Birdbath

As stained glass hobbyists for more than 20 years, we've collected a lot of scrap glass. We used some of it for this cardinal birdbath. It's made from 100 percent recycled materials, including an old satellite dish for the base, a tree stump for the stand and leftover supplies from our hobby.

If you don't have an old dish to use, buy a basic birdbath at the garden center. Then use a fine-point marker to draw the pattern, and secure the glass in place using hot glue. Be sure to leave space for grout later.

RANDALL & BLYTHE RICHARDS, *Winchester, Wisconsin*

Clever Faux Design

I like turning wine bottles into hummingbird feeders. I used stained glass paint to give the one here a mosaic look. Then I sprayed it with a coat of clear gloss finish, so it should last for a couple of seasons. You can find a feeding port like the one I used at most pet stores.

DEE FINN, *Pulaski, Virginia*

grow your own safflower

Plant this annual to delight cardinals, chickadees, jays and more. BY SALLY ROTH

Move over, sunflowers—there's a new seed in town. Safflower is easy to grow and provides your feathered friends with first-rate food.

The first time I found sprouting safflowers under my bird feeder in spring, I thought they were sunflowers. The seedlings look a lot alike, each stem sporting a pair of smooth green ovals. But the next leaves, the true leaves, told a different tale. They were deep, glossy green with sawtooth edges. So I was puzzled at the new sprouts.

Then I remembered I'd added safflower seeds to my feeder menu earlier that winter. The cardinals loved them. The seeds must have either fallen out of the feeder or been cached by jays. Either way, I had a little plantation going, and I couldn't wait to see the end results.

SAVING SAFFLOWERS. Like sunflowers, spent safflowers can be left in the garden for the birds to find on their own, or you can dry and hang the seed heads for them.

Time to Grow

Unlike sunflowers, these seedlings take their time. They produce a rosette of leaves and then stall for a few weeks. Meanwhile, an incredible taproot is growing underground, snaking 4 feet deep or more in a single season.

With a root like that, you'd think this would be a hardy perennial. But safflower's actually an annual: After the first hard frost in fall, it's dead as a doornail.

Safflower needs a growing season of at least 100 days to produce seeds, about the same as winter squash. If you can grow pumpkins, you can grow safflower.

Perfect Partners

Even if the birds don't plant it for you, safflower is simple to grow. Just poke some kernels from your seed mix into the ground in spring, about the time you notice sunflowers starting to sprout. Plant them about an inch deep in a sunny spot.

Safflower leaves get spiny as the plant matures. To save your fingers, grow the plant in a casual bed with blue larkspur, bachelor's buttons, cosmos, marigolds and other easy-care, self-sowing annuals where it can take care of itself.

The fluffy flowers bloom just in time to catch the last wave of butterflies—migrating monarchs, skippers, sulfurs and other nectar seekers still on the wing.

Once upon a time, most safflower blooms were a rich shade of orange, so deep the petals were used for dye. But today's varieties were developed for seed production, not color, so the blossoms may be orange, pale yellow, buttery gold or even red.

Keep the Birds Fed

Each flower holds just a few dozen seeds, but each branching, 2- to 3-foot-tall plant holds lots of flowers. By autumn, their ripening seeds will be packed with protein.

Even a small planting can keep cardinals, jays, chickadees, titmice, finches, native sparrows and doves investigating all fall and winter.

Come spring, you're likely to find some volunteers from seeds that got buried under the snow or fallen leaves. Want more? Just reach for the bag of birdseed.

cardinals love this seed!

AN ADDED BONUS. Though this seed is beloved by many favorite backyard birds, it's not sought after by squirrels and birds such as grackles, crows and blackbirds.

a plant to dye for

Though we use it today for birdseed or cooking oil, the dye from safflowers was once so prized that its botanical name, *Carthamus tinctorius*, says it twice. The first word is from the Arabic *gurtum*, referring to dye. The second is a form of the Latin word for dye.

nest box in an instant

Welcome robins and wrens to your backyard with recycled objects.

BY ALISON AUTH

One year a pair of Carolina wrens showed interest in making a home outside our sunroom. After witnessing days of indecision and debate, I thought I might help them along by installing a nesting box. (Wrens, robins and mourning doves are some of the many birds that use them readily.)

I chose a small galvanized bucket that I'd been using for years. It was perfect—not too big or too small, with sweet angled sides and a wire handle. Here's how I did it:

STEP 1. Paint the bucket. Painting is often the easiest way to transform the ordinary into something snazzy. I chose a pumpkin-orange spray paint for the outside of my bucket and metallic silver for the inside. If this bucket had been in newer condition, I would have left the inside unpainted.

STEP 2. Plan the attachment. I knew I was going to screw this bucket directly onto our porch column (made out of a tree trunk, courtesy of Hurricane Isabel in 2003), so all I needed to do was drill a hole in the center of the bucket. But if you think you might attach your nesting box differently, make sure it's ready to hang before accessorizing it with delicate objects.

STEP 3. Adorn the bucket. The shape of this little bucket reminded me of a head, which made me want to add a hat. I didn't want this topper to overwhelm the bucket, so I decided to use wire. I also like the way wire

7 more shelter ideas

BASKETS. Easter baskets, market reed baskets or small thrift store baskets are easily adorned with greens and decorations.

OLD MAILBOXES. A wall-mounted mailbox can be attached to a tree, under eaves or on a column, while a post-mounted model can be perched on a fence post or tree stump.

CARDBOARD BOXES. The right size cardboard box can be roofed with rubber or metal, sealed on the exterior with shellac or marine varnish, then decorated.

KITCHENWARE. Whether it's a copper garlic holder or a stainless steel pasta pot, don't overlook common household items. A cupboard or closet can be a gold mine of ideas!

GARDEN POTS. A terra-cotta pot already has a hole cut in the bottom. Add a screw and a washer, and it's ready for mounting. All you have to do is embellish it however you'd like.

OLD PORCH LIGHTS. We've all seen the nests in our porch lights. If you replace an old light, don't throw it away. Often, just a few adjustments make it display-worthy and bird-friendly.

PAINT BUCKETS. The 1-gallon metal kind is a nice size. Just make sure to hang it in a shady spot so it won't get too hot.

bends, and the fact that birds (unlike bigger critters) have no problem perching on it. The bucket's wire handle gave me an easy way to attach the hat.

STEP 4. Find a site and hang. When choosing a location, keep in mind that Carolina wrens and robins are the

most likely birds to take up residence in a nest box. Carolina wren nests are frequently found near homes, usually 3 to 6 feet off the ground, and in odd places. Robins' nests tend to be in the lower halves of trees, as well as in gutters or eaves, and on outdoor light fixtures and other structures.

easy-to-make birdbath

Put together this inexpensive birdbath in less than an hour. BY DAISY SISKIN

supplies

- 3 rods, each about 3 ft. long (either 1-in. doweling, ¾-in. metal electrical conduit or old broom handles)
- Exterior-grade paint
- Basin (preferably one with sloping sides, maximum depth of 3 in. and a textured surface for good footing)
- Hammer or mallet
- Piece of scrap wood

To attract birds this spring, I wanted to add another birdbath to my backyard. But like a lot of things, finding a birdbath that fits the bill and doesn't break the bank isn't as easy as it seems.

I knew what I wanted: something easy to clean, affordable, distinctive and attractive. What I decided on is a simple and versatile birdbath anyone can make.

STEP 1. Cut the rods to the needed length, depending on how deep you need to sink them into the ground for stability. If you have loose, sandy soil, you will need to sink them deeper than if the ground in your yard is primarily hard clay. I found the right length to be about 3 ft.

STEP 2. Paint the rods. If you're using metal conduit, be sure to wash them with a degreasing detergent to remove any oil and grime from manufacturing. Allow your work to dry completely.

STEP 3. Choose the location of your birdbath. A shady spot with nearby shrubs or trees for safe cover is ideal. For maximum enjoyment, make sure you'll be able to see the bath from your favorite bird-watching window.

STEP 4. Pound the rods into the ground in a triangle formation to provide a stable base for the birdbath. Using a piece of scrap wood between the hammer and the rods will cushion the blows. The size of your chosen basin will determine the distance between the rods.

STEP 5. Place the basin on top of the rods. Fill the bowl with water and check to see if the base is level. If not, adjust the depth of the rods until the water is level. Place a stone or two in the water to provide an extra perch for birds. Don't forget to clean and fill it regularly!

budget bird feeder

This tomato cage makes a sweet feeder! Add tin flowers, an arching plant and a colorful seed dish, and you'll soon have a work of avian-friendly art.

BY ALISON AUTH

Feeder Assembly

STEP 1. If you already have a location in mind, install your tomato cage there to start. You can either insert the tines into the earth as you would normally (the deeper and more even, the better), or bend the tines outward to form "feet."

STEP 2. Measure the circumference of the tomato cage ring that you want to use for holding up your plant. Arrange plants in a plastic pot with a top circumference slightly larger than the ring on the cage. Ease it down into place.

STEP 3. Measure the very top ring of the tomato cage for a plastic bowl or tray to rest there, and then scout around for a colorful receptacle that fits your dimensions. Your kitchen, yard sales and thrift stores are all ideal options.

STEP 4. Make the flowers. (See flower assembly steps.) Twist the wire stems around the vertical tines of the cage.

STEP 5. Last but not least, drop the bowl or tray into the top ring of the cage, and add birdseed.

Flower Assembly

STEP 1. Draw a simple flower shape on your choice of metal and cut two or more with tin snips or a similar metal-cutting tool.

STEP 2. Cut out one small center circle for every two flowers you cut.

STEP 3. Spray-paint flowers and circles in the colors of your choice.

STEP 4. Nestle two of the flowers together and place a circle on top

in the center. Using a nail and a hammer, punch a hole in the center of the flower cluster with a whack of the hammer on the nail. Repeat for the rest of the flowers.

STEP 5. Take about 12 in. of wire that is stiff enough to hold the flowers upright but flexible enough to bend easily. Using needle-nose pliers, twist a loop in the wire about 2 in. from one end. This will support the flowers so they don't fall straight down the wire.

STEP 6. Thread the flower cluster onto the short end of the wire to rest on the loop you made, and twist the wire above the flower into a spiral using needle-nose pliers. This will sandwich the flowers between loops so they are secure. Repeat for the rest of the flowers, and you're ready to attach them to the tomato cage.

$1 bluebird feeder

The early bird will get the worm with this simple tuna can feeder.

BY KRIS DRAKE

Save your money for mealworms! This bluebird feeder, made from tuna cans, costs less than $1 to make. You just need a few supplies and tools. Then hang it in a tree and wait for those blue beauties to arrive.

STEP 1. Clean out the cans and let them dry.

STEP 2. Drill three holes in the shape of a triangle both on the bottom and just below the rim of each can. Be sure the holes on the top and bottom line up so the feeder isn't crooked.

STEP 3. Next, it's time to paint the cans. I used acrylic paint in many layers, allowing the paint to dry between each layer. Then I accented with a gold color metallic pen. You can also use spray paint or permanent markers to create your own unique design.

STEP 4. When the painted cans are completely dry, spray them with a little bit of matte finishing spray.

STEP 5. Next, cut the wire that will hold the two cans together. Cut six pieces, 9 in. long, of 18-gauge wire.

Insert one wire into a hole near the can rim and twist a few times, leaving about 3 in. for decorative curling and 6 in. for hanging. Repeat for all wires and the other can. Leave the pieces unattached for now.

STEP 6. To make the hanger portion of the feeder, cut about 12 in. of 16-gauge wire. At one end, make a small loop and then fold the wire over to fashion a hook. At the other end, create an eyehook. (Depending on where you plan to hang your mealworm feeder, adjust the length as needed.)

STEP 7. For the decorative element under the hanger, cut a 12-in. piece of 16-gauge wire to loop and curl. Using the photo as a guide, form a figure eight in the middle of the wire, then curl each end in a spiral as shown. Thread a short wire through a bead, make eyehooks at each end of that wire, and use the beaded wire to attach the two pieces together.

STEP 8. Time to attach the cans together. Start with the bottom can. Place a bead on each wire stem,

insert the wires into the bottom of the top can and make a small loop at the end of each one to connect. Do the same with the top can, attaching each of the wires to the hanger.

STEP 9. You can add swirls, beads and any other decorative elements to the bottom of the second can. Using 4-in. pieces of wire, insert them through the bottom of the can and decorate as desired.

STEP 10. Finally, hang the feeder and let the bluebirds come in to dine!

supplies

- **2 recycled cans (tuna or cat food)**
- **16- and 18-gauge wire**
- **Beads**
- **Paint**
- **Needle-nose pliers**
- **Drill**

mealworms 101
5 sources for these wigglers

1. *Find them online.* You can have mealworms shipped directly to your house; some places even offer a live delivery guarantee.

2. *Go to a local bait shop.* You'll probably pay a bit more, but in a pinch, bait shops usually have them.

3. *Check out your nearby pet store.* Again, you'll pay more, but it's a convenient way to get worms quickly.

4. *Buy them dried.* You can buy dried mealworms online or just about anywhere you shop for seed. Best of all, they'll last for months!

5. *Raise your own.* Save dough by raising your own endless supply of mealworms. Look for a mealworm farm online to get started.

make a *birdbath* lamp

Turn an old lamp into a water park for your backyard birds.

BY ALISON AUTH

supplies

- Old lamp
- Painter's tape
- Spray primer and paint
- Wide, shallow bowl for bath
- Clear epoxy
- Ceiling light canopy (optional)

OK, I admit it. I am a hoarder of lights. Old lamps, ceiling fixtures, chandeliers—they all lend themselves beautifully to reinvention, and I simply can't resist their promises. In this case, a $1.99 thrift-store lamp said, "Birdbath, birdbath, birdbath!" until, after a few paces, I succumbed and handed over my two bucks.

This was truly a fast and easy project. One lamp, a few hours, spray paint and some epoxy just about did it. So keep your eyes peeled and your ears open at those Saturday morning yard sales. You never know when a lamp will speak to you!

STEP 1. Remove the socket and lamp shade support from the lamp and cut the cord at both ends to make it easy to pull through the lamp housing.

STEP 2. I added a ceiling light canopy (pictured above right) to the top of my lamp to offer more support to the bowl. This was simple to do, since a ceiling canopy already has a hole in the center, and the lamp has a screw and nut, making attachment super easy. You may need to add a washer if the nut on the lamp is smaller than the canopy hole.

STEP 3. It's much easier to paint the lamp before adding the bowl. Make sure to wash the lamp for a dust-free surface, and let dry thoroughly. I used painter's tape to protect the base of the lamp.

STEP 4. Several light coats of spray paint within a few minutes of each other provide a quick transformation.

STEP 5. When the paint is thoroughly dry, usually within an hour or two, you can glue the bowl onto the circular canopy edge. I used a clear epoxy out of the tube all around the bowl. Epoxy takes a while to set up but is extremely strong.

STEP 6. Make sure to mark or eyeball the center of the bowl before gluing it to the canopy. An off-center bowl will fall over when you fill it with water. Set the birdbath aside long enough for the epoxy to cure.

STEP 7. Scout the perfect spot, place the birdbath, fill it up with water and enjoy your handiwork!

CHAPTER 4

welcome, Wildlife!

Find out how to make your yard a habitat for the winged creatures you love to watch. Learn ways to lure migrators to your yard. Discover which multipurpose plants keep wildlife coming back.

ROBIN IN NEST, BILL LEAMAN

Common yellowthroat
on spiderwort

create the ULTIMATE *backyard habitat*

20 ideas to establish and capitalize space for your favorite backyard birds, bugs, butterflies and other wildlife.

BY STACY TORNIO

If you love birds, there's a good chance you're already planting, growing and gardening with them in mind. But there's always a way to do more.

So what's the best way to maximize your backyard for local wildlife? And how do you get more bang for your buck? We have the answers!

Now, keep in mind that it can take years for your yard to reach its full potential, so don't let our list overwhelm you. But that doesn't mean you can't make a difference now. For starters, pick three things on this list to implement this year—or more, if you're feeling ambitious. The birds, bugs, butterflies and other wildlife in your area will thank you.

INVITE WILDLIFE. Plant natives (like the marsh marigolds at top right) to attract wildlife. Also at right are a monarch feeding on native asters and a garden spider on a bidens bloom, both welcome backyard visitors.

Make a Difference Through Gardening

Start a new garden space just for wildlife. If you don't already have a designated bird or butterfly garden, now is the time to create one. You'll find entire books and websites dedicated to the subject, so look around, consult a few resources and start working on a space today.

Expand your canvas with containers. Don't have the space to start a whole new garden? No problem! Containers are a stylish solution. Hanging baskets add flair and offer a good source of nectar. You'll be amazed at some of the new containers on the market, especially the self-watering varieties.

Get rid of invasive plants. Start by going online to *plants.usda.gov* and clicking on Introduced, Invasive, and Noxious Plants on the left-hand side of the page. You can search by state to see some of the invasive plants in your area. Once you know what they are, remove them as soon as possible.

Plant more natives. While you're ridding your yard of invasive plants, replace them with natives, which almost always suit the needs of local wildlife. Planting natives suited to your growing conditions will feed and shelter birds, butterflies and many other creatures.

Lose some grass. Most American backyards sport more grass than any other plant. It may be overwhelming to think about shrinking your lawn by half, so don't go that far! Take it in stages instead. Put in a garden bed here and there. Before you know it, you'll have a slew of new wildlife-welcoming plants…and a lot less grass to mow!

Discover a new kind of grass. Try designating an area for ornamental grass. Beauties such as prairie dropseed and Karl Foerster feather reed grass will feed birds and offer four-season appeal. Group them together, and you'll start to have a whole new appreciation for grasses.

Never underestimate the value of a good tree. If you plan it right, a tree can offer multiple benefits to wildlife, including nectar in spring, nesting space in summer, and berries in fall and winter. Go ahead and invest in a new tree for your backyard. You won't be sorry.

Bring in the Wildlife

Serve a buffet. In addition to offering plants for wildlife, it's also good to put out different kinds of food. Of course, the birds and wildlife in your area will do just fine without it, but if you want an up-close view, this is the way to get it. Start by putting out black-oil sunflower seed and a sugar-water feeder. Then add items such as suet, thistle seed, safflower and peanuts as you like.

Check your birdhouses. Many commercial birdhouses are more decorative than useful, so be sure to do your homework. For instance, if you want to attract bluebirds, make sure you have a bluebird house with the right dimensions and hang it in the right area. Do a little research to learn about dimensions for different species before you buy or build.

Don't forget about the butterflies. Nectar-rich plants attract butterflies, so you have lots of options there. But don't neglect to provide host plants for their eggs and caterpillars, such as milkweed for monarchs. Look for butterfly garden resources near you.

Offer some water. Along with food and shelter, water is one of the three necessities of every backyard habitat. A larger water feature is remarkable, but at the least, consider adding a birdbath. Birds will flock to it, especially in the heat of summer.

Reduce pesticide use. When you have caterpillars, bugs, butterflies and young birds exploring your backyard in summer, the last thing you want is for them to be harmed by pesticides. Make an effort to reduce pesticide use for the health of wildlife.

BENEFITS IN EVERY CORNER. Plant containers with bird and butterfly favorites (left). Also, try native grasses (middle) and suet (right) to maximize your efforts.

do more, do less

Audubon's At Home program offers these simple ideas for enhancing your wildlife garden.

more

Bird feeders
Native plants
Water features
Nest sites

less

Turf lawn
Free-roaming cats
Invasive plants
Impervious hardscaping

Keep cats inside. It may be hard for cat lovers, but even our birding expert George Harrison, a cat owner himself, agrees with this tip. Cats are a leading cause of songbird deaths, so it's best if they stay indoors.

Think of the Big Picture

Set goals. Don't overdo it. Maybe your goal is to add three new native plants this year. Or maybe you have a more ambitious plan to start a whole new butterfly garden. Whatever it is, no matter how big or small, it's important to set goals each season and then follow through.

Turn your yard into an experiment. Citizen science projects such as eBird, Backyard Bird Count, NestWatch and more are looking for birders and gardeners like you to provide valuable data for researchers. Sign up to help benefit science for generations to come.

Get the whole family involved. Making your yard more wildlife-friendly will be a lot more fun if you can involve everyone in your family. Have a discussion early on about why you're doing this and what it means. Then note things to watch for and assign individual jobs.

Share your success with the neighbors. Rethinking your backyard is an excellent first step, but involving others is when you'll really make a change. Let them know why you're reducing your lawn or adding more feeders. If you can get a whole neighborhood involved, you'll see results much faster!

Devise a plan. A brand-new program from Cornell Lab of Ornithology makes it easier than ever to set specific goals for your backyard. Try out the new YardMap website, *yardmap.org*. It's an innovative approach perfect for creating a backyard haven for birds.

hummingbird habitat

Plant natives that hummers love. Bee balm, phlox and salvia are just a few of the perennials that hummingbirds can't resist. To attract these jeweled fliers, remember that natives are always best.

- Offer lots of red. It's definitely true—hummingbirds adore red. So be sure to plant enough red flowers to keep them coming back for more.

- Choose a combo that blooms from spring through fall. You don't want all your flowers to fade just when fall migration is starting. Plan carefully so that you'll always have something to offer. Or try some of our Top 10 suggestions for long bloomers (page 52).

- Migration time is key. Spring and late summer are big times for attracting hummingbirds. Even if you don't have regular summer visitors, don't give up just yet.

- Make sure your sugar-water feeders are always filled, so the birds stay around all summer. Visitors will lose interest in your yard if nectar runs out. And take care to change the sugar water regularly.

- Keep the water coming. Hummingbirds especially love mists (see our DIY mister project on page 64).

Take the pledge. Audubon At Home is a program of the Audubon Society, whose Healthy Yard Pledge supports the establishment of better wildlife habitats. Check out the quick list on page 91 and go online to *athome.audubon. org/healthy-yard-pledge* to learn even more. It's a handy checklist to keep you on track.

Certify your backyard. The National Wildlife Federation has one of the best-known programs with its Certified Wildlife Habitat, which allows you to pledge to provide food, water and shelter for the birds, butterflies and other wildlife in your yard. If you haven't yet certified your backyard (you probably already meet the requirements), now is the time. Go to *nwf.org* for more info.

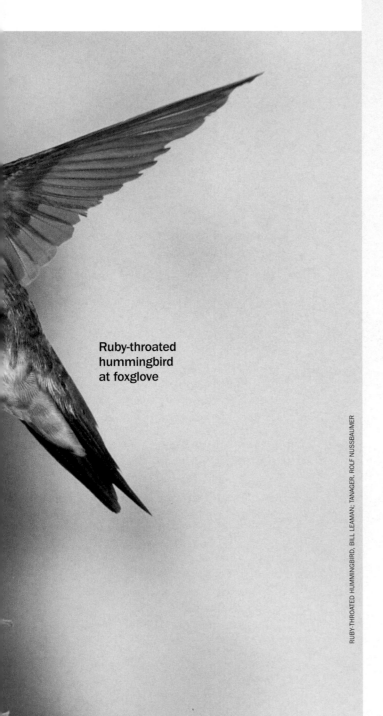

Summer tanager

Ruby-throated
hummingbird
at foxglove

Attracting Non-Seedeaters
BY GEORGE HARRISON

Go back to the basics to attract non-seed-eating birds to your backyard.

Non-seed-eating birds are more difficult to lure to backyards because they aren't interested in the food we offer in our feeders. In most regions of the country, we see these birds only in spring and summer; in winter, they migrate to warm climates where food is available.

So the question is, how can we get the non-feeder birds to show themselves? And how can we get them to come close enough so that we can enjoy watching them in spring and summer, too?

The simplest answer is to offer them water for drinking and bathing. All backyard birds need water in some form, and if we provide birdbaths, running pools and fountains, these non-seedeaters will come. Be sure that at least part of the water area is very shallow so that the birds can stand in it to bathe and drink. To do this, place stones in the middle or along the edges of the deeper water so that they're no more than 1½ inches from the surface.

The greater challenge is to offer these non-seedeaters a meal. American robins and American woodcocks eat earthworms; warblers, vireos and flycatchers eat insects; hawks, vultures and shrikes consume small mammals and birds. How do we get these birds to come to our backyards for dinner?

The best way is to give them plenty of natural cover from which they can hunt their preferred foods. A well-managed, bird-friendly yard will naturally host an abundance of insects, earthworms and larger prey to feed predatory birds. In other words, if we plant the right stuff, the non-seed-eating birds will also come.

for less

Help the nesting birds in your backyard this spring.

a helping hand

1. OFFER NESTING MATERIAL. Nest builders welcome your snipped thread and old yarn. You can even buy hanging nest aids—or make your own by filling up an old suet feeder.

2. PLANT SOMETHING SUBSTANTIAL. Every tree or shrub you plant will provide food, shelter and nesting spots. Add at least one. (Find an expert's favorites starting on page 104.)

3. PUT OUT A NEW BIRDHOUSE. Pick the style that suits the type of bird you're looking to attract. Our birdhouse guidelines are available on *birdsandblooms.com*. Many commercial birdhouses don't meet these standards, so make sure you buy one that does.

4. MONITOR NESTS. Keep tabs on the active nests in your backyard. Then, share your findings with a citizen science program such as Cornell Lab of Ornithology's Project NestWatch.

5. CREATE NEW NESTING SPOTS. Some birds, including robins, don't favor birdhouses, but you can still attract them. An old hanging basket or bucket makes the perfect platform for a nest. (See our project on page 78.)

6. FILL YOUR FEEDERS. Most parents are busy searching for bugs and worms for their young, but the adults need energy, too. Keep your feeders full, and consider adding mealworms to your offerings. Mom and Dad will appreciate the help feeding the youngsters.

7. KEEP YOUR DISTANCE. As tempting as it may be to look in on your backyard nesters, be sure not to get so close that you disturb the process.

6 THRIFTY TRICKS
for wildlife gardeners

Bring more birds and butterflies to your backyard all year—for less.

1 *Start small.* If you're new to wildlife gardening, test the waters first by planting a container garden filled with nectar-rich favorites such as lantana (pictured here), floss flower and fuchsia. As your confidence builds, convert more landscape.

2 *Build a pint-size pond.* A whiskey-barrel water garden is lovely to look at, easy to care for and a magnet for passing birds. Be sure to give feathered friends something to stand on while they bathe.

3 *Take advantage of late-season sales.* Many perennials, trees and shrubs are heavily discounted in autumn. Buy and plant wildlife favorites, and next year your yard will be more popular than ever.

4 *Rescue native plants.* When you see such plants (like the cardinal flower at left) on a local construction site, ask the developers if you can remove them before they're bulldozed. They're often happy to oblige.

5 *Nix insecticides.* Invite beneficial insects to your backyard. Maybe you'll see a bit more leaf damage, but it's worth it when you consider that many fliers, such as the wren at left, look at bugs as their favorite meal.

6 *Save on seed.* Fill your landscape with seed- and berry-bearing plants, such as sunflowers, viburnums and black-eyed Susans. When the time is right, birds will come a-flocking.

winter habitats

*Learn how to make your yard more wildlife-friendly,
especially during the coldest months of the year.*

BY DAVID MIZEJEWSKI

When it comes to making a garden more attractive to wildlife, most people automatically think about food and water. But it's the third component of habitat—shelter—that often makes gardeners scratch their heads, especially in winter.

Wildlife need shelter for two main reasons. The first is to hide from their predators—or, if they are predators themselves, to hide and wait for prey. The second is to protect themselves from harsh weather. Finding places

to do both is harder in winter, when landscapes lose their lushness and temperatures aren't kind. But there are ways you can help.

Power in Planting

First, think of native plants. The same ones that provide food also offer natural winter shelter. In fact, mature plantings of any kind provide shelter, so don't cut them down. In addition, try to add as many new plants as you can each year. Soon enough you'll

have lots of new places to protect wildlife in your own landscape.

How you design your garden matters a lot, too. A large tree might shelter canopy-dwelling creatures, but if you add smaller understory species, you'll provide homes for a different set of critters that prefer that layer of the woodland.

Plan your plantings for maximum benefits. Wildflowers and grasses in dense clumps can be used nearly year-round, especially when you leave them up in winter. For shrubs, consider planting them close together in a living fence instead of scattering them individually across the yard. You'll not only provide shelter, you'll offer a safe corridor across your yard.

Finally, remember that evergreens are the workhorses of the landscape, offering year-round shelter. If your space is limited, dwarf conifers are a good option.

Beyond the Garden

There are other ways to provide winter havens beyond your plantings. One of the best is to build a brush pile. Start by layering logs or large branches a few feet apart. Then layer successively smaller branches until you have a dome-shaped pile with chambers of various sizes inside where wildlife can hole up. Add a layer of dead leaves over the top to serve as insulation from the cold.

Some animals might even hibernate under brush or rock piles, including toads, lizards and mourning cloak butterflies. Hibernating frogs and turtles will use your water garden if it's large and deep enough, and if you allow a good layer of dead leaves to accumulate on the bottom.

You can also install roosting boxes (right) that will keep various birds and small mammals warm on those chilly nights. Roosting boxes look

OFFERING SHELTER. Shelter is an important part of bringing birds and wildlife to your yard. Left, a mourning dove finds protection from the wind in an evergreen. At right and below are a roosting box and a lushly planted yard, which both offer shelter.

something like birdhouses, but with some important differences. The entry hole should be at the bottom of the box, which helps it hold warmth, since heat rises. The interior should be studded with perches or have a ladder. This maximizes the number of critters that can fit inside, which is important because more bodies mean more insulation.

One last idea is to keep dead standing trees or hollow logs in your yard if you can. They'll quickly become a favorite with birds and other creatures.

If you make just a few of these changes, you'll probably discover that the winter landscape can be surprisingly alive with wildlife. By providing good winter shelter in your garden, you enhance your chances of seeing it.

feeding birds
year-round

**Bring more birds to
your backyard this
year with our simple
seasonal tips.**

BY ANNE SCHMAUSS

It used to be that most backyard bird-watchers fed their visitors only in winter. Times have changed, though, and birders are starting to realize how much fun it is to feed birds all year. To get more birds (and more kinds of birds) at your feeder this year, just follow these simple seasonal tips.

Winter

Not all birds head south in the winter. Lots of your favorites, like cardinals, chickadees, nuthatches and juncos, will stick with you through these cold, dark months and maybe even brighten your days a bit.

Birds flock to feeders in winter, especially during cold spells, heavy snows and ice storms. You'll want to use large-capacity feeders so you don't have to trudge through the snow as often to refill. Bring feeders up close to the house, since most of your viewing will happen from inside.

Keep those seed feeders filled with a mix of mostly sunflower and some white millet. Fill feeders in late afternoon so food is available just before nightfall and at daybreak, when birds need a boost after the long, cold night. Add an extra suet feeder to give woodpeckers and others another high-calorie dining spot in your backyard.

Thistle (nyjer) is a winter must. Pine siskins, common winter visitors, love this seed.

Spring

Springtime is when birds are most active. A wide variety of colorful songbirds are coming home to nest, while others are just passing through, so pull out all the stops by offering a banquet.

For seed, using a mix of black-oil sunflower, white millet and sunflower chips (sunflower seeds without the shells) will cover most of your spring bases.

WINTER FRIENDS. Northern cardinals are some of the most popular visitors during winter. Here, males and females share space at a feeder on a snowy day.

Chickadees, nuthatches, house finches and cardinals love sunflower, and so do migrating rose-breasted grosbeaks. The millet that falls to the ground might attract migrating white-throated, white-crowned and chipping sparrows. Sometimes even buntings show up at a feeder this time of year if it has some white millet.

Although insect eaters, including warblers and robins, can't crack shells easily, they'll eat sunflower chips. But by the time bugs become plentiful later in the spring, you probably won't see many warblers, buntings or tanagers at your seed feeders.

Suet is a favorite of woodpeckers all year, but in spring, tanagers, warblers, bluebirds and kinglets also relish this high-energy treat. Feed live mealworms to bug-loving new arrivals such as bluebirds, wrens, warblers, mockingbirds and robins. The mealworms are a nice high-protein snack.

Offering nectar in the spring beckons hummingbirds and even orioles. Here's a spring must: Display fresh orange halves, meat side up, on a spike or dead tree branch. Orioles and tanagers can't resist them.

Summer

Summer means lots of hungry young bills to feed, with some birds having as many as four or five broods of babies. Even though nature provides plenty of bugs, berries and seeds, it's fun to watch fledglings flap their wings, squawk and beg their patient parents for food at your feeders.

Young and old birds alike will continue to eat your seed mix if it's loaded with black-oil sunflower. Chickadees, house finches, sparrows, cardinals, nuthatches and more will bring their babies to your seed feeders for a lesson in finding a free lunch.

Suet eaters like woodpeckers are around all summer and love to bring the family over for a bite. Often, when you see several woodpeckers together at a suet feeder in the summer, you're seeing parents teaching their big, awkward babies where to find a snack.

Both seed- and suet eaters are attracted to seed cylinders if they're heavy on sunflower and nuts. These large cylinders last a long time and need little maintenance, making them perfect when you're away on vacation.

Goldfinches are sought after year-round but are bright yellow only in the summer. Feed fresh thistle all summer long to attract these beauties.

CHANGE IT UP. Adjust your offerings throughout the year to attract the most species of birds. From mealworms and fresh oranges in spring and summer to nuts in autumn, your feathered friends will love the variety.

Baltimore oriole

Eastern bluebirds

Red-breasted nuthatch

Summertime is hummer time, which means sugar water is a necessity. If you surround your feeder with honeysuckle, salvia or trumpet vine, you should see increased hummingbird action, especially in mid- to late summer as young ones join their parents at the feeder.

Autumn

Think of fall as spring migration in reverse, only with more birds, including young ones making their first trip south.

Feed a mix with sunflower, millet and chips to see some of the same migrants you spotted in spring. Watch for white-crowned, white-throated and chipping sparrows.

Warblers and kinglets might join the year-round woodpeckers and nuthatches at your suet feeder. The arrival of the juncos every fall is the highlight of the season for many. Juncos stick around all winter and love to eat millet from the ground.

Orioles may make a pit stop at your jelly or nectar feeder as they head south. Hummingbird activity often peaks in September as local parents and babies join migrants from farther north on the road to Mexico or Central America.

Year-round residents such as cardinals, woodpeckers, nuthatches, jays and chickadees are hunkering down for the winter and are looking for regular sources of food and cover to get them through the cold months ahead.

Keep your seed and suet feeders filled so your yard becomes a regular stop on their feeding circuit. Make sure your seed feeder has enough space so larger birds such as cardinals and grosbeaks are comfortable. A hopper feeder, tray feeder or tube feeder with a tray all work well.

You might consider adding a ground feeder this time of year, too. Also, freely toss seed mix loaded with millet on the ground in several places around your yard. Lots of juncos, migrating sparrows and towhees can spread out to eat with plenty of elbow room.

SEASON-LONG APPEAL. Native grasses have lots to offer, such as nesting material in spring, a treat for caterpillars in summer and seeds for birds in fall and winter.

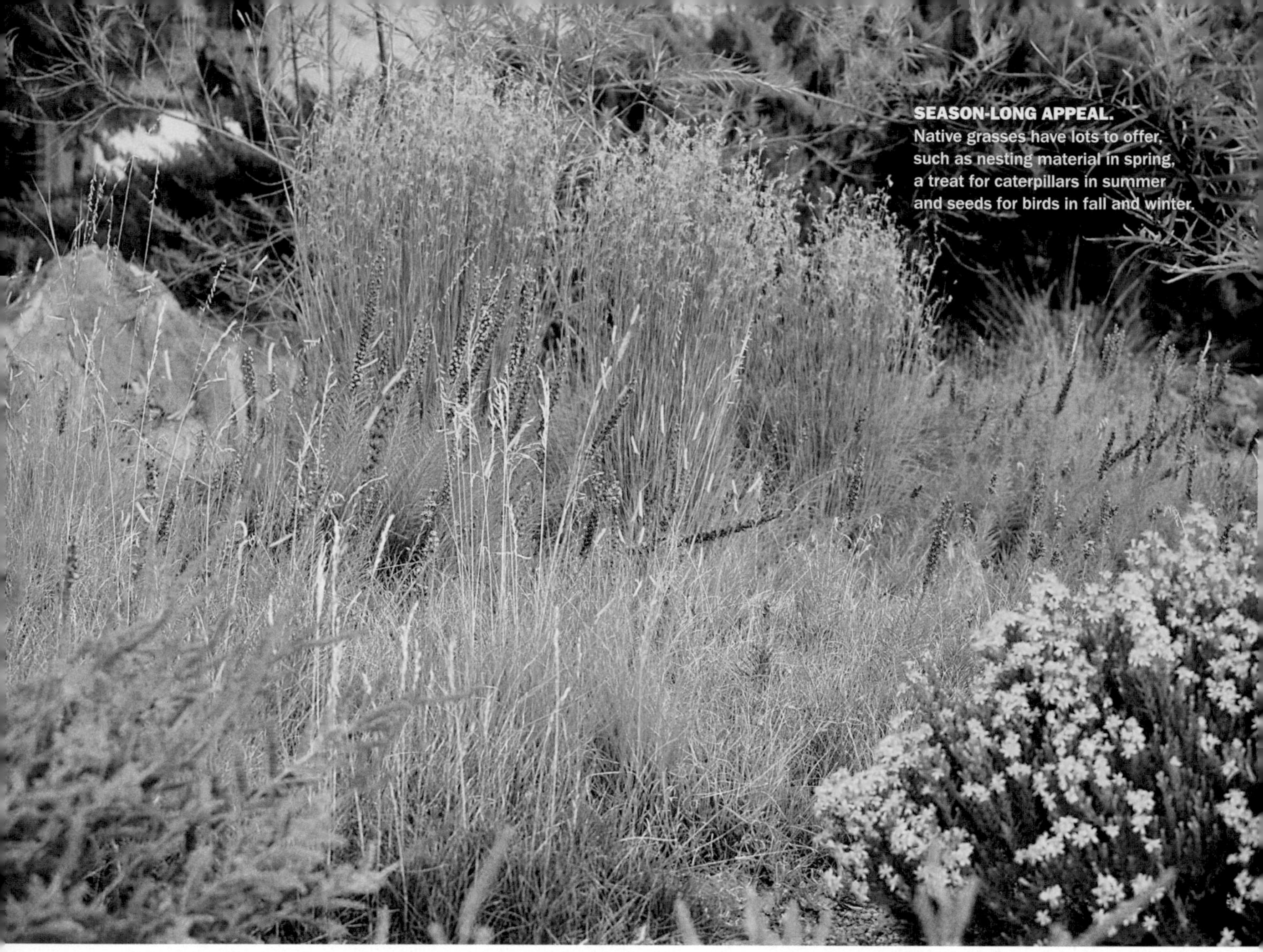

naturally native

Plant native grasses and watch your yard come alive with birds and butterflies.

BY SALLY ROTH

Ornamental grasses are full of life. They sway in the wind, bow beneath snow and rustle with a music all their own throughout the seasons.

Keep an eye on those graceful clumps and you'll see life of another kind, too. Birds and butterflies love them. Native sparrows, finches and other small birds forage for seeds from grasses in the garden, just as they do in the wild. And more than 100 butterfly species, especially skippers, use certain grasses as host plants.

With so many kinds of ornamental grasses on the market, and new ones joining them every year, how's a gardener to know which ones are best for birds and butterflies? It's simple, really. Go native!

Benefits to Birds

Birds visit all North American native grasses, thanks to the nutritious morsels on the plumes, spikes or sprays. For juncos, native sparrows, buntings and other seed-eating birds, it doesn't matter what part of the country the grass is originally from.

Many natives, including Indian grass, big bluestem and switchgrass, are already garden favorites as ornamentals, both in their original form and in variations like the Heavy Metal cultivar, which is a cool shade of blue-gray.

Don't expect to see your ornamental grasses nodding under a bustling flock of hungry goldfinches, though. Instead, look for finches, native sparrows, juncos, doves and other birds hopping around on the ground beneath the plants in fall and winter, scratching for fallen seeds or stretching for overhanging seed heads.

9 native picks for birds

When you cut back your ornamental grasses in early spring, pile clippings where you can keep an eye on them. Nest-building birds will soon spot the freebies-for-all. Try these top growers.

Big bluestem (*Andropogon gerardii*)

Blue grama grass (*Bouteloua gracilis*)

Indian rice grass (*Achnatherum hymenoides*)

Little bluestem (*Schizachyrium scoparium*)

Muhly grass (*Muhlenbergia* spp.)

Northern sea oats (*Chasmanthium latifolium*)

Prairie dropseed (*Sporobolus heterolepis*)

Sideoats grama (*Bouteloua curtipendula*)

Switchgrass (*Panicum virgatum*)

European skipper

Year-Round Attraction

In spring, when nesting season arrives, any and all grasses may be the focus of birds' attention. Dead grass, that is.

Dry grass is lightweight, plentiful, easy to maneuver around and a cinch to collect. Birds aren't fussy about what they use in their nests, as long as it's strong and flexible.

Robins, song sparrows, wrens and other birds use blades of coarse grass, such as miscanthus, for the main wall of the nest. The dead leaves of other fine-textured grasses often serve as part of the soft inner circlet that lines the nest.

Grasses come into their glory as summer arrives, and that's when delightful grass skipper butterflies take an interest in them, too. This big subfamily includes about 140 species, all with a definite predilection for grasses as host plants.

So go ahead and add a few grasses to your backyard. Fall is still a good time to plant them. You'll be well on your way to attracting even more birds and butterflies to your space.

Baird's sparrow

a birder's guide to
growing berries

BY KEN KEFFER

Plant these 12 picks now for fliers to feast on later.

I admit I'm not a huge gardener. I appreciate working the soil, and I like growing my own food, but I'm much stronger in the birding area of this magazine than in the blooms. As a naturalist, though, I know there's a lot of value in gardening for wildlife.

Gray catbird
in dogwood

There's something inspiring about seeing a cheery flock of cedar waxwings suddenly settle into your backyard, stretching to pluck every berry within reach. They gulp the fruits down one after another before leaving as quickly as they arrived.

You can revel in this picture-perfect scene, too. Not only are berries among the most natural and essential food sources for birds, they're also easy to grow. Translation: You don't have to be much of a gardener to achieve success!

Take a look at my top 12 picks for backyard berries, compiled with the bird-watcher in mind. (My editor made me add the botanical names.) All are easy to grow in small spaces, yield good crops and will bring birds to your backyard for years to come. From one birder to another, I hope this advice allows you to simply plant, walk away and then get your binoculars ready to enjoy the view.

BLACKBERRY (*Rubus fruticosus*). If you have the space, plant them in thickets. Birds will spend countless hours camped out, gorging themselves on the crop. It's really fun to watch chickadees munching away on blackberries the size of their heads!

BLUEBERRY (*Vaccinium*). Since these beauties generally require moist, well-drained acidic soil, some gardeners prefer to use them as container plants. Robins and bluebirds will feed on them, and indigo buntings look especially at home with their blue feathers among the ripe berries.

DOGWOOD (*Cornus*). Several species are native to North America,

and upwards of 40 kinds of birds have been documented eating their berries. One of my favorites is the gray catbird, whose long tail and stubby wings are perfectly suited for flying through dense dogwood thickets. The plant is available as either a small tree or a bush.

ELDERBERRY (*Sambucus*). A hit with many birds, from wrentits to flycatchers, purplish-blue elderberries grow in clusters. If you somehow can harvest the berries yourself before the birds devour them, they make a delicious pie filling, jam or syrup.

HOLLY (*Ilex*). What's more festive than holly's bright-red berries clustered among dark-green leaves? Although the fruit can be mildly toxic and irritating to humans, birds seem to have no problem with it. Research suggests that the berries lose some of their toxicity after the first frost, which is when birds tend to chow down on them. Another thing to know about holly: It's dioecious, meaning you need to have both male and female plants to ensure that fruit will be produced.

HUCKLEBERRY (*Gaylussacia*). A relative of the blueberry, huckleberry is equally popular with birds. I prefer to enjoy it in ice cream form, but the birds love it right off the bush.

BAYBERRY (*Myrica*). While most warblers are spending the winter in Central and South America, flocks of the yellow-rumped species remain in the southern United States all winter long. Many species of bayberry, including wax myrtle, provide fruit for the warblers. In fact, the eastern subspecies of the yellow-rumped warbler is often referred to as the myrtle warbler.

CURRANT (*Ribes*). Many currants produce fragrant flowers and abundant fruit. Except for a few species, the berries are largely unpalatable to people, but the birds will thank you for planting these treats in your backyard. A bonus: Hummingbirds are wild about the flowers.

JUNIPER (*Juniperus*). Any of the juniper species can offer double benefits for birds, providing good

Yellow-rumped warbler eating bayberry

THEY LOVE IT ALL.
Cedar waxwings aren't
choosy when it comes to
berries. They'll snack on
just about all the varieties
on Ken's list as well as
these pyracanthas.

cover and choice nesting locations as well as fruit. These berries are especially popular with the Townsend's solitaire; while they're less appealing to some other birds, they still provide valuable winter nutrients. And for the wildlife gardener, these hardy shrubs need minimal maintenance.

VIBURNUM (*Viburnum*). With around 150 different species, this is a versatile choice for your backyard berry patch. These shrubs can do well clumped as a hedgerow. They also make a good transition species at a forest's edge. The berries are favorites of both birds and larger wildlife.

RASPBERRY (*Rubus idaeus*). I used to find towhees and sparrows in my raspberry patch every morning when I'd go out to harvest some berries for my pancakes. The dense patches provide excellent cover, and sometimes the birds refused to flush from the thicket as I picked a few treats for myself.

SERVICEBERRY (*Amelanchier*). Most of these species bloom early and then quickly yield berries prized by numerous birds, including vireos. It's easy to find serviceberry shrubs at garden centers. Some serviceberries are considered small-scale trees, but they don't grow too large, so both tree and shrub work nicely in smaller landscapes.

Plant any of these choices, and watch the show begin! A flock of waxwings can make short work of a berry buffet, while a northern mockingbird will vigorously defend a berry patch to hoard the pickings, enjoying them at a leisurely pace. Either way, when you plant berries, you'll have a front-row seat to some fascinating bird behavior all year long.

Scarlet tanager eating pokeweed berry

THE SKY IS THE LIMIT. While these are Ken's top berry picks, don't limit yourself. See what works in your area. You might find that a shrub like pokeweed (left) or a tree like this mountain ash are best for your backyard.

American robin in ash tree

Chipping sparrow
on spruce

top trees for wildlife

Get the most bang for your buck by planting these native favorites.

BY DAVID MIZEJEWSKI

When it comes to choosing plants with the most long-term benefit to the wildlife in your backyard, you can't go wrong with native trees.

Of course, what's native to one area might not be native to another, but all those I've listed here have species across North America. It's just a matter of finding the right species for your yard.

Whether you plant large canopy trees or smaller understory species, they all provide height and structure to the garden and offer layers of habitat to maximize backyard wildlife. For instance, warblers, flying squirrels and orioles will hang out in canopies,

while chickadees, screech-owls and Steller's jays are more likely to be found in understories.

Trees provide homes for decades or even centuries. They also offer a whole buffet of food options in the form of seeds, fruit, nuts, sap, nectar, leaves, pollen and insects.

Not all trees are created equal when it comes to attracting wildlife. But if you carefully select the ones you plant, you can provide food for a variety of species, along with shelter and places to raise young. So give these trees a try. Remember to do a little research to find the species or cultivars that will thrive in your climate and soil conditions.

American goldfinch
on willow

MAPLE (*Acer*). Birds and small mammals devour the seeds within the winged samaras of maples. The leaves also make these trees host plants to almost 300 butterfly and moth species.

BIRCH (*Betula*). Many birch species have beautiful white, black or tan bark, and their conelike strobiles are a food source for birds and small mammals. Birch is the host plant for more than 400 species of butterflies and moths.

SPRUCE AND PINE (*Picea* and *Pinus*). Spruce and pine offer excellent year-round shelter and produce seed-filled cones that beckon birds and small mammals. Pines are the host plants for more than 200 butterflies and moths; spruce for more than 150.

POPLAR (*Populus*). Songbirds, waterfowl and small mammals love to feed on the cottony seeds of these trees, and more than 350 butterflies and moths eat its leaves.

CHERRY, PLUM AND CHOKECHERRY (*Prunus*). The fruit ranges from tiny black cherries to inch-long American plums, and songbirds, ground birds and mammals of all sizes relish it. Plus, more than 400 moth and butterfly species eat the leaves.

OAK (*Quercus*). The acorns feed everything from squirrels and deer to wild turkeys and black bears. More than 500 butterflies and moths are attracted to this host plant.

WILLOW (*Salix*). Willow seeds feed a wide variety of songbirds, waterfowl and small mammals. The trees are host plants for more than 400 butterflies and moths.

Mourning cloak on birch

Orchard oriole on maple

Western tiger swallowtail on cherry

Black-capped chickadee
Photo by Eric Carr / Alamy

Crabapple blossoms
Photo by Michael Lustbader

Pearl crescent resting on an aster
Finalist in our Backyard Photo Contest
Photo by Mary Rabadan

American goldfinch on thistle
Photo by Max Allen / Alamy

Four baby house wrens
Photo by Glenn and Linda Miller

CHAPTER 5

breathtaking Blooms

Plant enchanting and easy-care perennials, annuals, shrubs and trees. Keep your tools and to-dos organized with clever ideas from green thumbs. Discover what type of landscape suits your personality best.

GAP PHOTOS / JULIA BOULTON

gardening MUSTS

shoulds

& coulds

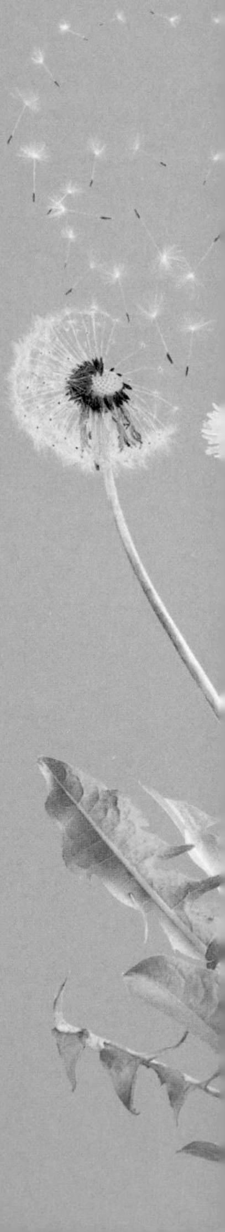

Busy gardeners appreciate
this three-tiered approach
to writing to-do lists.

BY SUSAN MARTIN

Gardening can be relaxing, therapeutic and a perfect way to enjoy some exercise outdoors. But it can also be a lot of work. And since most of us have jam-packed schedules, we have to pick and choose how to spend our time.

I understand this dilemma and have developed a way to maximize results in the garden. I call this the "must-do, should-do, could-do" model. I broke it up by level of importance, starting with crucial gardening tasks and moving on to less essential ones. Try it, and see if it doesn't help you juggle your busy summer!

must
- water your plants
- control weeds

Must-Do

You must water your plants to keep them alive. I know it sounds simple, but it's also easy to forget. If your region gets less than an inch of rainfall per week, you'll need to provide supplemental water for most of your plants, especially annuals, which require even more moisture.

Drought-tolerant perennials will not be as thirsty as others, but they aren't completely carefree. Pay special attention to things you have recently planted; they'll require extra water the first year as they are getting established.

I recommend to gardeners that they water deeply and less often, rather than watering a little bit every day. Deep watering encourages the roots to grow deeper down into the soil where moisture naturally resides, making the plant more self-sufficient.

You have to control the weeds in your garden. It's too easy to let them get out of hand, so stay on top of them early.

Weeds rob vital nutrients and water from desirable plants. So make it a weekly routine to pass through the garden and pull any weeds you see right away. It's amazing how fast they can grow!

Should-Do

You should feed your plants for optimal results. Think about it: You enrich your soil when you first establish your garden, but those nutrients don't last. The plants use them, so you need to replenish.

The best way to feed your plants is through the soil. When you add nutrients there, the roots take them up to feed the rest of the plant. An easy way to do this is to add an inch or two of compost on top of your garden bed each fall. Top with a layer of shredded leaves that will decompose during the winter, and you'll have soil ripe for planting in spring.

Doing this alone will provide enough food for most perennials. But if you still want to provide additional fertilizer during the growing season, use organic rather than synthetic products whenever possible.

Divide some of your perennials every few years. One of the best things about perennials is that they continually increase in mass. So after a few years, they naturally need to be divided and replanted again.

It's easy to tell if you need to divide a perennial. There's a bare spot in the center, the flowers are smaller than usual and less prolific, or the plant has overgrown its allotted space.

The best time to divide most perennials is in the spring, when the foliage is just starting to emerge. There are a few exceptions, though. Spring bloomers should be divided in the fall, and tall bearded irises should be divided in late summer when the weather starts to cool.

Mulch your garden in spring and/or fall. A 3-inch layer is ideal. Sensitive, less cold-hardy perennials will benefit from an extra-deep layer of mulch going into winter, especially in climates with unreliable snow cover.

should

- feed your plants
- divide some perennials
- mulch your garden

Could-Do

Now for the "coulds." Don't think these aren't important just because they come last. Sure, your garden is going to be fine if you don't do these things, but you'll have an even better one if you do.

Stake your perennials to give them support. Some tall perennials such as delphiniums and peonies really should be staked so their stems don't break. This is especially important in windy, exposed sites. The plants will still live if you don't, but you'll get a longer life out of the blooms if you do.

Deadhead the spent blooms on your perennials. This will instantly improve the look of your garden—and it can be a relaxing task. Some perennials will even reward you with a second round of blooms. But even the ones that do not bloom again will benefit because they don't spend energy on developing seeds and can focus on root development instead. That means they'll be stronger than ever the following year.

Pinch or cut back your perennials. Some, such as garden mums, benefit from being pinched back periodically to maintain their compact form—if you don't do this, they'll likely start to look unkempt. The general rule where I live, in the Midwest (though this will vary by zone), is that you can pinch the plants back until Independence Day without sacrificing flowers in the fall. If you time it right, a new flush of growth will quickly replace the flowers and foliage you've cut back, leaving the plant looking lush and full.

Good luck! I hope these simple ideas help you create a better garden in less time!

could

- stake some perennials
- deadhead spent blooms
- cut back some perennials

1

shrubs for small spaces

Yes, you do have room for an extra shrub or two—all of our picks are under 5 feet tall!

BY STACY TORNIO

You have a very small backyard, perhaps just a patio, yet you still want to grow shrubs. Or maybe you have a good-sized yard, but it's filled to the max. Your significant other has even made threats that start with: "If you buy one more plant, I'll…." Or perhaps you just like miniatures because they're so darn cute!

It doesn't matter what your story is; nearly everyone can find a use for a small shrub. So many kinds are available that it may seem impossible to choose just one or two, but you'll certainly have fun trying. Use our top 10 picks as your guide to the best of the best.

1

Sapphire Surf bluebeard

(*Caryopteris* x *clandonensis*, Zones 5 to 9)
Many perennials will outgrow this small shrub, which is just 2 feet tall. Grow it as an accent plant, or group several together for a bigger impact. It blooms endlessly in full sun.
WHY WE LOVE IT: You can't beat these blooms. The purplish-blue flowers are absolutely gorgeous.

2

Garden Glow dogwood

(*Cornus hesseyii*, Zones 4 to 8)
Dogwood comes in many shapes and sizes, so consider adding a compact variety to your backyard. This Garden Glow cultivar is true to its name, with neon-bright foliage. It grows only 3 or 4 feet high and prefers partial sun.
WHY WE LOVE IT: In addition to those glowing leaves, its red winter stems give it four-season appeal.

5

Hummingbird Summersweet clethra

(*Clethra alnifolia*, Zones 4 to 9)
Clethra is a popular shrub known for its fragrance, shade tolerance and bright summer blooms. Most clethras grow 8 to 12 feet, but now you can have this beauty in your own small space with this compact version, which reaches only 2 to 5 feet.
WHY WE LOVE IT: It will tolerate full shade—ideal for gardeners with lots of dark areas in their backyard.

6

Bella Anna hydrangea

(*Hydrangea arborescens*, Zones 4 to 9)
Some hydrangeas grow tall while others are compact, but all boast beautiful blooms. The pink Bella Anna is fairly new to the market, and it has gardeners excited. Grow it in full sun to partial shade; it reaches up to 3 feet. Pay close attention to plant labels for other small-space hydrangeas.
WHY WE LOVE IT: A hydrangea with pink blooms. Need we say more?

9

Dwarf bush honeysuckle

(*Diervilla lonicera*, Zones 3 to 7)
You won't have to worry about disease or insect problems with this honeysuckle shrub. It's very hardy, even in cold climates, and can take dry, sandy soils as well. It grows up to 4 feet tall, with green foliage that changes to red in fall. Look for the variegated cultivar Cool Splash.
WHY WE LOVE IT: It's similar to honeysuckle without invasive problems, and it's a prolific summer bloomer.

10

Dwarf fothergilla

(*Fothergilla gardenii*, Zones 5 to 8)
Growing just 2 to 3 feet tall, these bushy, low-growing shrubs are striking when grouped together along a border in full sun or partial shade. Look for showy blooms in spring, green leaves in summer, and yellow, red and orange leaves in fall. Blue Mist is a cultivar with blue-green foliage.
WHY WE LOVE IT: You'll get three-season appeal with this beauty.

3

Cranberry cotoneaster

(*Cotoneaster apiculatus*, Zones 4 to 8)
With pink flowers in early summer, fruit in late summer and bronze foliage in fall, this plant shines for months. It grows just 2 to 3 feet tall and has dense foliage.
WHY WE LOVE IT: In addition to all that color, the birds will love the abundant berries.

4

Scarlet Beauty sweepspire

(*Itea virginica*, Zones 5 to 9)
If you're looking to save a lot of space, look for the Little Henry sweetspire cultivar, growing just 18 to 24 inches high. For a little more height and lovely fragrant blooms, go for Scarlet Beauty (pictured here). It grows 3 to 4 feet.
WHY WE LOVE IT: The shape of the flowers—long 3-inch panicles—is distinctive and delightful.

7

Goldflame spirea

(*Spiraea* x *bumalda*, Zones 4 to 8)
You can find a slew of compact spirea, but this Goldflame cultivar is one of our favorites. It starts off with bronze new growth, which matures to a yellowish green in summer. Then come the summer flowers, and after that the leaves turn orange in fall. Grow in full sun.
WHY WE LOVE IT: With its changeable, brightly colored leaves, it's not your typical shrub.

8

Lo & Behold butterfly bush

(*Buddleia*, Zones 5 to 9)
This new noninvasive butterfly bush comes in cultivars Purple Haze and Blue Chip. Both are compact, growing only 2 or 3 feet tall and wide, making them a perfect choice for gardeners who love the blooms of butterfly bush but don't have much space. They prefer full sun.
WHY WE LOVE IT: Whichever cultivar you go with, the flowers are heavenly, blooming from summer to frost.

tips for small spaces

These days, it seems as if there's a dwarf version of nearly everything. Here are some additional tips for finding smaller varieties.

BROWSE A LOCAL BOOKSTORE OR LIBRARY for small-space gardening books and jot down the names of your favorites.

USE LOCAL EXPERTS, such as the staff at your garden center or Master Gardener volunteers, to ask them for recommendations for small spaces.

LOOK ONLINE at plant companies you trust. We love Bailey Nurseries (*baileynurseries.com*), an excellent source for shrubs. The company even provided most of the photos for this story. Proven Winners is another good place to check out (*provenwinners.com*).

SEARCH THE WEB. Google your favorite plant but add "dwarf" in the name as well. Examples: dwarf conifers or dwarf sunflowers. Be sure to check the size, though. Some dwarf varieties might not be as small as you'd think!

garden
more
water less

Learn how to choose water-wise plants that defy heat and drought.

BY NOELLE JOHNSON

Drought-tolerant garden. What do you think of when you hear that phrase? A stark and sandy landscape punctuated by cactus or other spiky plants? An arid expanse in uninspiring shades of brown?

If that's what you envision, you'll be surprised to learn that drought-tolerant gardens can be filled with beautiful flowering plants, trees and succulents adapted to survive on very little water. And you don't have to live in the Southwest to add these plants to your backyard. After all, who doesn't want to save a little time and money on soaking, sprinkling or hosing? Learn how to pick suitable plants, and then start gardening more and watering less!

The Benefits

Drought-tolerant plants come in endless shapes and colors. Dazzling flowers, fascinating foliage, striking shapes—you can have it all while watering it very little.

Surprisingly, drought-resistant plants often don't need much other maintenance, either. Some do fine with no fertilizer, while others need just a modest amount. And they don't sport much excess growth, so pruning is minimal as well.

Selecting Plants

As with any garden, native plants are a good place to start. But you may also be tempted by options from the drier regions of Australia, Africa, the Mediterranean, or Central and South America.

Group together plants with the same water, temperature and sunshine needs. No matter how pretty they may look together, don't make the mistake of pairing a drought-resistant plant with one that needs lots of water. Wet soil can kill a desert plant. Plant your new acquisition in native soil, mixed with compost to boost the water retention of sandy soil and to help heavy soil drain excess water.

Water Basics

Just because a plant has desert origins doesn't mean it can thrive without water forever. It especially needs water in its crucial first year. Although many drought-tolerant plants can eventually survive on only rainfall, they'll look better with regular watering.

The key is to water them deeply but infrequently, allowing the soil to dry out between soakings. Trees should be watered to a depth of 3 feet, shrubs up to 2 feet deep and perennials about 1 foot deep. This encourages the root system to grow deeply and become well established.

Not sure how deep the water's going? It's easy to test this in your garden with a piece of rebar. Simply push it into the soil near your plant after you finish watering to measure the depth.

Using drip irrigation or a soaker hose is an efficient way to water slowly, which allows moisture to penetrate the soil without runoff. Plants also do best when watered early in the morning, which lets the roots drink deeply before the water evaporates in the heat of the day.

How often you water will depend on the weather conditions, of course. To determine when your drought-tolerant plants need a drink, simply stick a trowel in the ground 4 inches deep. If the soil is moist, your plants are fine.

Additional Tips

Want to save even more water and grow lusher plants? Use mulch around those drought-resistant beauties. Not only does it slow down evaporation, it cools the soil and helps prevent weeds.

You might also consider planting living "mulch" in the form of drought-tolerant ground covers around your other plants. It will do many of the useful things that bark chips, shredded leaves and other conventional mulches do.

Ready to plant your own low-maintenance, drought-resistant garden? Try it, and who knows? Maybe your neighbors will catch on, and you can start conserving water in a big way!

GAP PHOTOS / JERRY HARPUR / DESIGN: MARY EFFRON

Noelle's Drought-Tolerant Plant Picks

ANNUALS
Cosmos
Gazania
Marigold
Nasturtium
Vinca
Zinnia

SHRUBS
American holly
Beautybush
Bush dalea
Butterfly bush
Japanese barberry
Juniper
Privet
Rosemary
Russian sage
Texas sage

PERENNIALS
Angelita daisy
Bearded iris
Bachelor's button
Blackfoot daisy
Butterfly weed
Candytuft
Coneflower
Coreopsis
Damianita
Daylily
False indigo
Gaura
Lamb's ear
Lavender
Lilyturf
Monarda
Penstemon
Salvia
Verbena

TREES
Afghan pine
Acacia species
Chinese pistache
Desert willow
Hackberry
Honeylocust
Live oak
Mesquite
Pomegranate
Texas mountain laurel

SUCCULENTS
Agave species
Argentine giant
Euphorbia
Yucca

1

colorful succulents

These easy-care gems will surprise you with their displays of sun-drenched yellows, reds, oranges and more. BY LORIE WEST

Succulents, where have you been all my life? Browsing through Debra Lee Baldwin's enticing *Succulent Container Gardens*, I fell just a little bit in love. These plump-leaved plants store water in their juicy tissues, making them a forgetful gardener's dream. Give them well-drained soil and plenty of sun, and your succulents will look as healthy when you return from vacation as when you left. In fact, they may look even better.

That's because stressors that might harm or even kill other plants—an extra touch of sun, heat or cold; even a drought resulting from the gardener's vacation—make many succulents come alive with color. Normally green and blue-green leaves heat up into a vivid spectrum of reds, oranges, pinks, purples and yellows. Another bonus: Succulents tend to be winter bloomers. So when you bring your frost-tender plants inside to protect them from the cold, you'll get a flower fix just when you need it most.

Easy care, a host of hues to choose from and winter flowers: Are you ready to become a sucker for succulents, too?

DROUGHT-TOLERANT CHOICES · OVERWINTERING TIPS · CONTAINER SELECTION

Succulent Container Gardens

Design Eye-Catching Displays with 350 Easy-Care Plants

Get more info on inspiring container combinations, design ideas and plant care tips in *Succulent Container Gardens* by Debra Lee Baldwin.

1

Sticks on fire

(*Euphorbia tirucallii*)

With a thicket of loosely branching vertical stems, each about the diameter of a pencil, sticks on fire looks almost like something growing on an undersea reef. Also called red pencil plant, it has tips that turn yellow in summer and red in winter. Beware: When broken or damaged, the stems ooze sap that may irritate skin.

WHY WE LOVE IT: Height and shape make this the perfect thriller in any container, while the changing colors ensure a fabulous show.

2

Baby's necklace

(*Crassula rupestris* subsp. *marnieriana*)

The stacked geometric leaves of baby's necklace prefer some sun protection, yet will still reward you with a rosy blush. In winter, pretty white blooms emerge from the ends of the leaf strands.

WHY WE LOVE IT: When planted front and center in a container, the strands of leaves turn upward like eels, making baby's necklace a fun three-dimensional spiller.

5

Paddle plant

(*Kalanchoe luciae*)

The flat, round leaves of this succulent—also known as desert cabbage and flipping flapjacks—can grow up to 6 inches in diameter. They begin to blaze red from their tips downward, growing more vibrant with additional sun or cold. From late winter through early spring, pale-yellow blooms open, a pleasing contrast to the fiery leaves.

WHY WE LOVE IT: The color and pattern of the leaves make this a simply spectacular plant.

6

Morning Light echeveria

(*Echeveria* 'Morning Light')

A succulent this stunning must be hard to grow, right? Nope! This cultivar is among the most user-friendly you'll find. Preferring a soil slightly richer in organic matter than most succulents, it flourishes under ultrabright indirect light.

WHY WE LOVE IT: Gorgeous powdery leaves splay open like a water lily or lotus blossom—but this echeveria's "flower" is always in bloom.

9

Coppertone stonecrop

(*Sedum nussbaumerianum*)

The trailing cylindrical leaves of this beauty turn a magnificent gold in the summer sun. Pure-white flowers bloom early, from January through April.

WHY WE LOVE IT: Between the winter blooms and the summer leaves, this sedum brightens gardens and windowsills year-round.

10

Red salad bowl

(*Aeonium urbicum rubrum*)

Aeoniums prefer a little more shade and humidity than the typical succulent, but they're still some of the easiest blooms to grow. The large, well-defined rosettes of this red-and-green aeonium will add class to your containers.

WHY WE LOVE IT: It has the bicolor charm of the popular Green Envy coneflower, but it's colorful all year long.

3
Golden tooth aloe
(Aloe nobilis)

Dark-green leaves with white or yellow prickles bake into hot colors under direct sunlight. But peek at the shaded surfaces underneath and you'll find tender greenery. Grow a golden-toothed and you'll be spoiled for plain aloe vera.
WHY WE LOVE IT: Vibrant red-orange flowers shoot up on slender stems during summer, offering nectar your hummingbirds will find hard to resist.

4
Royanum hens-and-chicks
(Sempervivum tectorum 'Royanum')

Why settle for plain old hens-and-chicks when you can have a gorgeous chocolate-tipped Royanum? A frost-tolerant, cold-climate succulent, it can be safely grown outdoors from Zones 4 to 9.
WHY WE LOVE IT: Coordinate your container to match the tips' hue, and you'll be amazed how the colors pop.

7
Fire and Ice
(Echeveria subrigida 'Fire and Ice')

Wavy tapered leaves overlap to form rosettes roughly a foot in diameter. Coloring ranges from blue-green leaves with red-purple margins to sea-foam-green leaves edged with dark pink.
WHY WE LOVE IT: When backlit, the slightly translucent quality of the leaves becomes apparent, and the red margins glow neon bright.

8
Sunset jade
(Crassula ovata 'Hummel's Sunset')

Especially during the cooler months, this cultivar's leaves take on bright golden centers with ochre margins. From late fall to winter, look for white flowers tinged with lavender.
WHY WE LOVE IT: In shade, it masquerades as its plainer green cousin, the common jade plant. What's more fun than a plant with a secret identity?

stress: too much of a good thing?

Succulents have adapted to grow in unforgiving territory: rocky soil, drought conditions and full sun. Most—particularly those with fat, fleshy leaves—can last weeks or months without water, even when exposed to hot sun, nipped by frost or rooted solely in gravel. Healthy reactions to these conditions are leaves that turn red, orange, gold, purple or pink. But how much is too much?

Beige, brown or gray leaves, especially if they're shriveled, mean the plant is suffering. If there's visible damage or they sustain prolonged stress—eventually, they all need a respite—move your succulents to a milder location.

Also, pamper them by watering to provide moist (not soggy) soil until they return to greener shades. You'll have healthier plants and more dramatic color changes the next time you stress them.

hang a
garden shed organizer

Who thought getting organized could be so much fun? Here's a project you can personalize that'll keep your yard on track for the long haul!

Hang this multifunctional wall organizer in your shed or garage to help with all of your spring, summer and fall gardening chores. Use the suggested items or look for your own hooks, boxes and materials.

STEP 1. Lay out all six of the 35-in. pieces of lumber side by side, spacing them about ¼ in. apart. This will form a 24- x 35-in. backing. Position the remaining 1x4s across each 24-in. end of the backing. Attach crosspieces with screws to every horizontal board.

STEP 2. Attach the cookie sheet, galvanized ledge and decorative hook along the top of the workstation or wherever you think they'll fit best. (In the organizer pictured, the ledge was mounted upside down as a shallow tray.) Fasten a double layer of cork tiles beneath the tray by nailing it in place every 4 in. around the edge. Mount the towel bar along the bottom.

STEP 3. Center the metal label holders on the boxes and lightly tap the prongs with a hammer. Insert labels to say whatever you want, such as "indoors," "spring" and "summer" for seed storage. Glue the wooden boxes and clothespins to the workstation base, following the directions for the construction adhesive. Allow the adhesive to dry overnight.

STEP 4. Hang the finished potting shed organizer by threading braided picture wire through a pair of sturdy eye screws.

supplies

- Six 1x4 pieces of lumber (35 in. each)
- Two 1x4 pieces of lumber (20 to 24 in. each)
- 1 cookie sheet
- 2 cork tiles
- Three 4½-in.-square wooden boxes
- 3 metal label holders
- 1 galvanized ledge
- 1 towel bar
- 1 decorative hook
- 4 spring clothespins
- Hooks, pushpins and magnets
- Electric chop box or hand saw
- Screwdriver
- Hammer
- Wood screws and nails
- Heavy-duty construction adhesive
- Eye screws and braided wire for hanging

Project courtesy of
Handmade Garden Projects
by Lorene Edwards
Forkner. Buy it for $19.95
at *timberpress.com*.

1

top 10 coneflowers

With dozens of new coneflowers on the market, learn how to pick the best for your backyard.

BY STACY TORNIO

Ah, coneflowers. How can you not love 'em? After all, they feed the birds, offer some of the longest-lasting blooms around, and are naturally drought-tolerant. To choose the top coneflowers, we teamed up with Great Garden Plants (*greatgardenplants.com*). This online plant company in Holland, Michigan, is definitely up on the latest coneflower trends. President Mary Walters helped us narrow down the latest and greatest echinaceas in several categories. Consider adding one (or 10) of these showstoppers to your garden.

1

Best Yellow: Sunrise

(Zones 4 to 8)

Bring a little sunshine into your garden with this buttery yellow coneflower. It will bloom up to eight weeks in your perennial garden; as it flowers, the petals fade to a soft white.

ALSO TRY: If you want to turn it up a notch from the softer shades of Sunrise, look for Harvest Moon. And if you want to turn it up one more notch, consider Maui Sunshine.

2

Best Double Bloomer: Pink Double Delight

(Zones 4 to 8)

Pink Double Delight took what people love about coneflowers and multiplied it! The pink pom-pom blooms make a big impact in the garden, and they're fragrant, too.

ALSO TRY: Marmalade is a nice option, especially if you need a break from pink. The blooms are a mix of orange and yellow.

5

Best Unique Color: Green Envy

(Zones 3 to 9)

Is it green? Is it pink? Actually, it's both, and it'll stop flower fanatics in their tracks, with fragrant blooms that are bright pink in the center and lime green on the tips. It has a long bloom period, too, so it's definitely worth a try.

ALSO TRY: Double Scoop Orangeberry was a new variety for 2012. It claims to carry more than 30 two-tone blooms per plant, and birds and butterflies love it.

6

Best Orange: Tangerine Dream

(Zones 3 to 9)

If you're a gardener who likes to make a statement, this plant is a must-have for your garden. Given a little time, it will reach heights of more than 30 inches, with mounds of pumpkin-orange blooms. To top it off, the flowers have a strong, spicy fragrance.

ALSO TRY: Tiki Torch has a fade-resistant orange shade with more upright blooms. Coral Reef's interesting centers help it look lovely in bouquets.

9

Best Classic: Magnus Superior

(Zones 4 to 8)

Now you can have the best of both worlds—the classic coneflower shape and color along with the added benefits of newer varieties. Fragrant and drought-tolerant, this beauty blooms from early summer through fall. If you need to replace any of your current classic coneflowers, this is the one for you.

ALSO TRY: Hope is another variety worth checking out. The coloring is a lighter pink, but it has the classic shape, and a portion of the proceeds goes to Susan G. Komen for the Cure.

10

Best Green: Green Jewel

(Zones 4 to 8)

Want a true green flower? Look no further—Green Jewel has large 4-inch flowers that get even greener as the flowers age. It grows up to 2 feet tall and wide, with more than 20 blooms per plant.

ALSO TRY: Coconut Lime is really a mix of green and white flowers. This double-blooming variety sports white petals below and pom-pom-like greenish blooms above. Every garden should have one!

3

Best White: Virgin

(Zones 3 to 8)

Virgin is really the cream of the crop when it comes to white coneflowers. It has very full, fragrant blooms with an upright habit, so it doesn't require staking.

ALSO TRY: Fragrant Angel definitely delivers the fragrance. Hummingbirds and butterflies love the full blooms, and the plant thrives in heat.

4

Best Unique Form: Raspberry Truffle

(Zones 4 to 8)

Another double bloomer, this coneflower sports enormous 3-inch-wide flowers. It first became available in 2011, and gardeners are already impressed with its performance, endurance and unique coloring.

ALSO TRY: Double Decker looks as if it has another set of blooms growing from the cone of the main flower. If you want unique, it delivers.

7

Best Compact: PowWow Wild Berry

(Zones 3 to 8)

You'll get a lot of bang for your buck with PowWow Wild Berry. It's only 24 inches tall, but produces many giant blooms on each stem—and they keep coming for up to five months.

ALSO TRY: Little Annie is so cute, you'll want to pinch its petals! It grows only 6 to 9 inches tall, making it just right for containers.

8

Best Red: Sombrero Salsa Red

(Zones 5 to 9)

One benefit of new coneflower varieties is that they produce more blooms on each branch. This is definitely the case with Sombrero Salsa Red. Its abundant deep-red blooms will steal the show for more than three months.

ALSO TRY: Red Knee High has a bit of a classic look with deep, rich bloom color. It's also compact, so try it in tight places.

the benefits of coneflower varieties

- Drought-tolerant once established
- Sturdy stems keep flowers from flopping
- Butterflies love them
- Superb cut flowers
- Highly deer-resistant
- Long bloom period
- Fragrant
- Easy to grow
- Improved flower color

what's your
garden style?

Use your backyard to express your personality.   BY SUSAN MARTIN

What does your garden say about you? Do you lean toward the traditional or the contemporary? The elegant or the informal? The homey or the sophisticated? Maybe you like to mix it up a bit and combine a few different styles together. With nearly as many garden styles as there are personality types, there's sure to be one that suits you to a T. Take a look at these 11 and find the best fit for you.

1. Asian

The natural tranquility of an Asian garden offers the ideal space for relaxation and reflection. Water, stone and artifacts are often combined with greenery. The emphasis is on the rich greens and browns of the natural landscape, with bursts of other colors here and there from specimen plants or sculpture.

PLANT PICKS: Japanese maples, Japanese painted ferns (*Athyrium*), mosses, ground covers such as Japanese spurge (*Pachysandra*), lilyturf (*Liriope*), bamboo, azaleas and evergreens.

2. Formal

Formal gardens have a well-defined structure of uniform, symmetrical plantings. Taking inspiration from geometric shapes, the garden's lines are usually straight and angular, leading the eye to a focal point in the landscape.

Symmetrical elements may include two identical borders flanking a patio, or two matching pots on either side of an entrance.

PLANT PICKS: You can use just about anything, but a limited number of plants lends a more formal effect. Instead of planting 20 kinds of perennials, as you might in a cottage garden, limit yourself to three or four and repeat them throughout the design.

3. Modern or Contemporary

Modern gardens have a clean, serene look about them. Their lines are similar to those used in formal gardens; they are based on geometrical shapes, with straight lines rather than soft curves. Bold colors serve as accents. The focus is on "hard goods" such as retaining walls, patios,

THE RIGHT FIT. Is Asian (left), formal (above) or eclectic (below) more your style? Read and find out!

outdoor furniture and sculptures. Materials such as glazed tile, stone, concrete and metal are commonly used as well.

PLANT PICKS: For a contemporary-style landscape, limit the number of plant varieties you use. Grow several of one kind in one area, with a pop of something really distinctive in the mix.

4. Eclectic

Eclectic gardens feature a blend of styles. A formal clipped hedge may enclose a cottage-style garden filled with rambling roses and climbing clematis. A shady woodland garden could border a patio filled with combination containers. The possibilities are limited only by your imagination.

PLANT PICKS: There are no boundaries! Mix and match, making sure you check light and soil conditions first.

5. Prairie

Though most native Midwestern prairie land has been converted for other uses over the past century, there has recently been a renewed interest in its restoration. If you'd like to create a traditional prairie garden, choose a flat or gently rolling plot of land that gets full sun. Enrich the soil with generous amounts of organic matter, but be sure it drains freely. If you don't have enough land for a traditional prairie garden, you can group prairie plants together in a smaller garden.

PLANT PICKS: Little bluestem (*Schizachyrium*), blue Indian grass (*Sorghastrum*), coneflowers (*Rudbeckia* and *Echinacea*), false sunflower (*Heliopsis*) and blue false indigo (*Baptisia*).

6. Cottage

Often characterized as free-form or random in their design, cottage gardens have an informal, welcoming air about them. The entrance may be gated, with a vintage arbor overhead and vines scrambling to the top. Combinations of annuals, perennials, bulbs, vines, herbs and roses are planted close together, and the garden is typically enclosed by a hedge, fence or wall.

PLANT PICKS: Hollyhocks (*Alcea*), delphiniums, peonies (*Paeonia*), daisies (*Leucanthemum*), foxglove (*Digitalis*), columbine (*Aquilegia*) and lamb's ear (*Stachys*).

A LITTLE BIT OF THIS, A LITTLE BIT OF THAT. While there are many different gardening styles to choose from, you can mix them, too. Cottage (left), container (above) and water (right) could all be in one backyard.

7. Container or Patio

In the past few years, container planting has become one of the top gardening trends in the U.S. You can use all kinds of containers to brighten up patios, decks, porches and balconies. Achieve a dramatic effect by using a single variety to fill a large container. Or to switch things up, change plants from season to season.

PLANT PICKS: Anything goes. You can grow only annuals and replace them every year. Or add some perennials. Overwintering perennials in containers takes a bit of skill, but it's worth the time to learn how.

8. Woodland or Shade

If you have lots of shade, you might choose to work with your existing landscape and plant perennials that thrive in this environment. You'll have lots of choices. Though many are grown for their interesting foliage, some perennials also flower well in shade.

PLANT PICKS: Hostas, ferns, foamflowers (*Tiarella*), astilbe, brunnera, bleeding heart (*Dicentra*), Lenten rose (*Helleborus*) and lungwort (*Pulmonaria*). Look for shade-gardening books at the bookstore or library for even more great picks.

9. Water

Water gardens, which have become very popular in the past decade, are usually man-made features that combine a pond with aquatic plants and ornamental fish. The key to a beautiful water garden is integrating it into the surrounding environment so it looks like a natural feature of the landscape. Bog plants thrive in water gardens. They grow with their roots underwater and the rest of the plant above the surface.

PLANT PICKS: Sweet flag (*Acorus*), rush (*Juncus*), Louisiana iris and cardinal flower (*Lobelia cardinalis*).

10. Rain

Rain gardens are healthy for the environment because their purpose is to slow, capture and filter polluted runoff water before it seeps into the ground. Instead of heading directly into storm drains and then into lakes and rivers, the water is naturally cleaned as it is filtered through the soil. Rain gardens should be located in areas where runoff is a problem, such as next to the street, at the roof's edge or alongside a driveway. Make sure you keep them away from the foundation of your house. Also, be sure the garden dips at the center so water can collect there.

PLANT PICKS: Native and cultivated plants tolerant of occasional flooding and drought are perfect for rain gardens. A few to try are sweet flag (*Acorus*), Joe Pye weed (*Eupatorium*), Siberian iris, swamp milkweed (*Asclepias incarnata*) and cardinal flower (*Lobelia cardinalis*).

11. Rock

You can plant a rock garden on a naturally rocky slope, or fabricate your own by importing rocks into the landscape. Elevate the garden by layering rocks and soil, taking care to position the rocks so they control erosion and allow pockets for planting. Typical plants are those that are naturally adapted to rocky or alpine environments and poor, well-drained, drier soils.

PLANT PICKS: Hens-and-chicks (*Sempervivum*), pinks (*Dianthus*), candytuft (*Iberis*), rock cress (*Arabis*), sea pinks (*Armeria*), Silver Mound artemisia, creeping phlox, creeping thyme (*Thymus*) and stonecrop (*Sedum*).

1

leave-'em-up plants

*Keep these perennials in your garden all winter long,
and the birds will thank you for the extra food source.*

BY STACY TORNIO

Didn't get around to cleaning out those flower beds this fall? Now you can justify it—not only is it good for your plants, but it's also a great food source for the birds! I'll admit I personally use these excuses a little too often to put off autumn chores. Keep in mind that you will need to remove any diseased plants, but leaving the others up actually increases the chance of the plants' winter survival. And with snowy days and freezing nights, your feathered friends are looking for food just about anywhere they can get it, so they'll appreciate the extra food the plants provide. Here are our top picks for "leave-'em-up" perennials.

1 Allium

(*Allium*, Zones 2 to 10)

If you want to add a colorful bounce to your garden, there's no better bloomer than allium. This pretty perennial is a winning selection for almost any yard. Not only can you find alliums to suit almost any spot, the enchanting plant is also easy to grow. Different types bloom from late spring to fall.

WHY WE LOVE IT: The dried flowers are like huge balls of seeds. Birds can't miss them!

2 Black-eyed Susan

(*Rudbeckia*, Zones 3 to 9)

This garden favorite ranges in height from 1 to 6 feet, and it delights birds from late summer through winter, or until all the seeds get picked clean. It multiplies fast, so start off with just a few. You'll soon have a large cluster of natural bird feeders.

WHY WE LOVE IT: It works well in just about any situation, whether you group it or use it as a background.

5 Sedum

(*Sedum*, Zones 3 to 10)

You can buy find both summer and fall blooming sedum. One popular type of this versatile succulent is Autumn Joy, with its broccoli-shaped flower heads. Most sedum peak in fall, bringing in late insects looking for a nectar treat. Then the plant continues to offer seed through winter.

WHY WE LOVE IT: It's easy to find and hardy in most climates.

6 Blanket flower

(*Gaillardia*, Zones 3 to 10)

This flower does it all, offering long-lasting color in summer and fall, brightening up bouquets and yielding seeds that you can save to plant or pass along to friends.

WHY WE LOVE IT: The beautiful flowers come in multiple shades, and the plant stays sturdy into winter.

9 Aster

(*Aster*, Zones 3 to 8)

A popular cut flower, the aster brings an explosion of color to the end of the growing season. From miniature alpine plants to giants up to 6 feet tall, it will brighten up fall in any backyard. And don't look past the small flowers: Birds love them for food!

WHY WE LOVE IT: Hundreds of varieties give gardeners plenty of colors to choose from.

10 Switchgrass

(*Panicum virgatum*, Zones 4 to 9)

This easygoing, versatile grass is a good choice for most landscapes. It tolerates drought and prefers full sun, but will tolerate partial shade. Growing tall, switchgrass can easily reach more than 5 feet.

WHY WE LOVE IT: It's a North American native and, like most grasses, it's attractive in a winter garden.

3 Bee balm

(Monarda, Zones 3 to 9)

While it's best known for bringing in the butterflies and hummingbirds in summer, it's also relished by seedeaters later in the season. For cultivars that resist mildew, try Marshall's Delight or Jacob Cline.

WHY WE LOVE IT: Its unusual shape stands out in the garden from summer all the way through winter.

4 Coreopsis

(Coreopsis, Zones 3 to 11)

With new varieties of coreopsis, you can now have this perennial in shades of pink, red and the traditional yellow. A champ in dry areas, some grow up to 4 feet tall.

WHY WE LOVE IT: You get lots of blooms for your buck, which translates to lots of food for your birds!

7 Coneflower

(Echinacea, Zones 3 to 9)

This native plant attracts attention from summer till the next spring. Plant it in a sunny space and put off cleanup until the snow melts. A bunch of the prickly seedpods will add a big architectural element to any winter garden.

WHY WE LOVE IT: The whole plant holds its shape well. Even when the snow piles on top, the sturdy stems won't fail.

8 Goldenrod

(Solidago, Zones 3 to 9)

Be aware that goldenrod can be a bit aggressive, so be sure to plant it near other assertive plants to maintain some balance or plant a tamer cultivar. If you can find the perfect place for it, you'll love it. It keeps lovely golden shades through fall and then has good winter structure as well.

WHY WE LOVE IT: This native favorite also grows abundantly in the wild, so it's an ideal natural food source for fliers.

buying plants online

Although the experience is less personal, there are benefits to buying plants on the web. BY MELINDA MYERS

My favorite place to shop for plants is the garden center. It's like walking through a living catalog where you can touch, smell and feel all the items. But if you're looking for new, heirloom or hard-to-find varieties, the only place to locate them might be online, where you can shop anytime you'd like. Here are a few I like to visit.

TROPICALS. Logee's (*logees.com*) offers a wide range of interesting tropical fruits and flowers for warm climates, patios and indoor gardens.

FRUIT. Grandpa's Orchard (*grandpasorchard.com*) carries both

heirlooms and some of the newer hard-to-find varieties, like the Zestar! apple. Stark Brothers (*starkbros.com*) has been a longtime provider of fruit plants for the home gardener.

SUPPLIES. Gardener's Supply Co. (*gardeners.com*) is the gardener's toy store. They carry composters, shredders, garden art, colorful plant supports, containers and a wide variety of items to help your garden and yard look their best.

SEEDS. Seed Savers Exchange (*seedsavers.org*) not only provides a wide selection of heirloom seeds,

but it also works to save North America's diverse garden heritage.

BULBS. Brent and Becky's Bulbs (*brentandbeckysbulbs.com*) sells traditional favorites, as well as unique offerings. Holland Bulb Farms (*hollandbulbfarms. com*) features the iMyGarden app to help with planning your bulb gardens.

Whichever site or catalog you decide to use, make sure the plants you buy are suited to your climate and will be shipped to you at the proper planting time for your area.

gardening
glad you asked!

Plant Doctor Melinda Myers is here to answer some of your toughest questions!

Watering Woes

I love succulents like aloe vera, cactus, hens-and-chicks and what many refer to as mother-in-law's tongue. How often should I water them, and how much water should I use? It seems no matter what I do, my plants turn mushy.

CONNIE COMER, *Levelland, Texas*

Melinda: Cacti and succulents grow best in full sun and well-drained soils. Drier soils and cooler temperatures in winter will keep these plants growing their best and will encourage spring blooming. Always water thoroughly, pour off excess water when growing in containers, and wait for the top few inches of soil to dry before watering again.

New Fruit

I've had this plant for 15 years, but I was surprised to see that it recently produced fruit. What is this shrub?

NANCY CORLEY
McDaniels, Kentucky

Melinda: Your spring-blooming shrub is a longtime favorite known as flowering quince (*Chaenomeles*). Hardy in Zones 4 to 9, it flowers best in full sun but will tolerate partial shade. The tart, yellow-green fruit is often used in jams, preserves and baked goods.

▼ A Close Relative

This plant grew from seed last year. I have a cockscomb (*Celosia cristata*), and it resembles that. Is it related?

CATHY LUCENT, *Arab, Alabama*

Melinda: Good observation. This is one of the so-called wheat types of celosia (*Celosia spicata*). Its finer texture lets it blend more easily with other flowers. Give this celosia the same care as your cockscombs. Grow in full sun and well-drained soil.

The Problem Corner

A corner of our yard floods every spring and during heavy rainfalls. But when the weather is hot and sunny, it gets very dry. What can I plant there that will survive these conditions?

DOROTHY ERICKSON, *De Pere, Wisconsin*

Melinda: Consider putting in a rain garden. First, make a depression in the area where the water collects. Amend the soil to improve drainage during heavy rainfalls and help retain water during drought. Then fill the area with plants that tolerate short periods of flooding and drought, like elderberry (*Sambucus*), swamp milkweed (*Asclepias incarnata*), turtlehead (*Chelone glabra*), sedges (*Carex*), purple coneflower (*Echinacea*), liatris and Joe Pye weed (*Eupatorium*).

Storing Bulbs

Can I store Japanese iris bulbs this winter until I'm able to plant them in the spring?

MARIE JUDD, *Thompsonville, Illinois*

Melinda: If the rhizomes—the fleshy underground stems we call bulbs—are still firm, you may be able to keep them alive. Pack the rhizomes in peat moss and store in a cool, dark place, like a spare refrigerator. This will keep the plants from sprouting until you can plant them outdoors after frost in spring.

▲Milkweed Seeds

During my morning walk in the woods, I discovered some butterfly milkweed. I would like to collect seeds in the fall to plant in my garden. When should I collect them, and where should I store them over the winter?

ROBERT DOLLEVOET
Combined Locks, Wisconsin

Melinda: Always ask permission before collecting plants and seeds on public or private land, and make sure the plant is not endangered or threatened. Butterfly weed readily self-seeds but is on the protected or at-risk list in some states, mostly in the Northeast.

Consider asking a gardening friend if you can collect seeds from one of his or her butterfly weed plants. Select pods in late summer or early fall, just as they are starting to crack but before the seeds are released. Milkweed seeds need a cold treatment to germinate, so immediately plant the seeds in your garden or pack them in moist sphagnum moss and store for 10 weeks or more in your refrigerator. Plant seeds outdoors in late spring, or start them indoors in warm, moist soil. Seeds will germinate in two to three weeks; move the transplants into the garden after the danger of frost has passed.

Go Away, Earwigs!

I am bombarded with earwigs each spring, in my garden and even in my house. I tried a spray and a powder from the garden center, and they didn't work. Any other suggestions?

MABLE PELLETIER, *Allagash, Maine*

Melinda: These pests eat harmful insects, which makes them both a friend and a foe to gardeners. You may want to try making a homemade, eco-friendly trap.

Fill the cardboard tube from a roll of paper towels with straws and cover one end and the outside with packing tape. The earwigs will crawl inside the straws during the day.

Each morning, knock the insects into a can of soapy water. Rolls of damp newspaper, crumpled paper under a terra-cotta pot, and bamboo tubes will also work.

▲Texas Night Bloomers

My mother-in-law gave me a few of these plants several years ago. She called them Texas night bloomers, but I can't locate any information for them. Can you help me identify this plant? They bloom every night just after dusk and shrivel and die off once the sun comes up. This process repeats all through the summer and into fall.

CHRIS CARLSON, *Rockford, Illinois*

Melinda: These cheerful night bloomers are also known as yellow evening primrose (*Oenothera*). They grow best in areas that have full sun and well-drained soil, especially during the winter. Include these night beauties in evening, rock and perennial gardens.

FAQ

"What can I plant in order to have a beautiful garden all year?"

Melinda: Look for plants with multiple seasons of interest and those that are suited to your growing conditions. Crape myrtle (*Lagerstroemia indica*) has beautiful flowers and multicolored bark that's appealing in every season. Redtwig and yellowtwig dogwoods (*Cornus*) brighten up winter landscapes. Don't forget about perennials, especially ornamental grasses that provide motion and texture throughout most of the year. Also try evening primrose (*Oenothera*), balloon flower (*Platycodon*) and hosta for excellent fall color. Coral bells (*Heuchera*), yucca and bergenia have stunning foliage in fall and even winter in many areas.

Dahlias
Photo by Mark Turner

Bachelor's button blooming
Finalist in our Backyard Photo Contest
Photo by Cindy Skeie

Grass pink orchid
Photo by Carol Freeman

Lily of the Nile
Photo by Linda Ried

Tulips
Photo by Mark Bolton / Getty Images

CLIVE CHAMPION / PHOTOGRAPHER'S CHOICE / GETTY IMAGES

CHAPTER 6

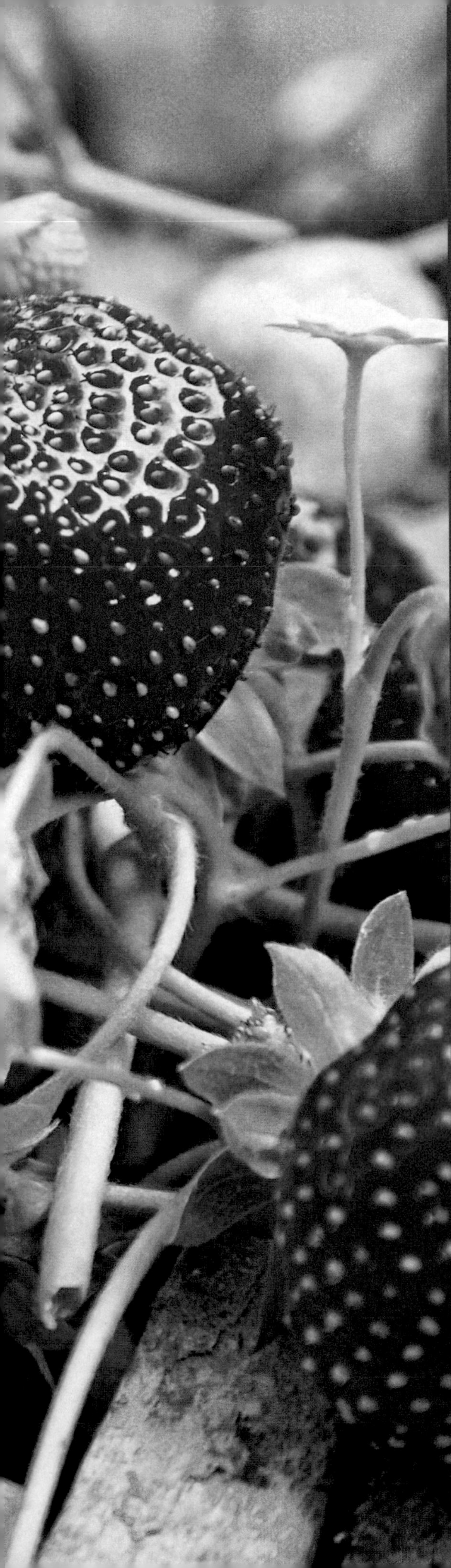

Incredible *edibles*

Boost the growing power of your fruits, veggies and herbs. Enhance your vegetable patch with simple structures that boast both form and function. Start seeds with no fuss.

the
heirloom
revolution

*From purple carrots to magnificent melons, these
historic varieties couldn't be hotter (or tastier).*

BY KIRSTEN SWEET

Long gone is the notion that a tomato should be red. Thanks to
the growing popularity of heirlooms, we see orange, purple, green
and even black tomato varieties adding interest to seed catalogs,
garden centers, farmers markets and some grocery stores.

Heirlooms are all the rage, and it's not hard to understand
why: When you plant and nurture them, you're growing a piece
of history. Gardening becomes special when you know you're
sowing the same seeds your ancestors did, long before hybrids
and pesticides were introduced.

You can find heirloom varieties of just about any fruit or
vegetable—carrots, lettuce, potatoes (one type of spud even has
purple flesh!) and so many more. Heirloom flowers and herbs are
also popular with gardeners.

Make this the year you plant at least one heirloom in your
backyard. You won't be disappointed.

So what exactly is an heirloom anyway?

The truth is, there's no official answer. Some say in order to be considered an heirloom, a cultivar must have been introduced before 1951, when plant breeders began to grow hybrids. But others say a true heirloom dates back even further than that, to at least the 1920s.

Kathy McFarland of Baker Creek Heirloom Seeds in Mansfield, Missouri, says her company doesn't use a cutoff date. As long as the variety is old and has been passed down from generation to generation, Baker Creek considers it an heirloom.

It's the same for Seed Savers Exchange, an organization dedicated to the preservation of heirloom seeds. Rather than use an arbitrary year, it identifies an heirloom by the documentation and generational history of a seed.

It's not just about dates, though. Most important, in order to be an heirloom, a variety must have been open-pollinated—that is, self-pollinated or pollinated by insects, birds, winds or other natural mechanisms while still maintaining its characteristics. Keep in mind, though, that not every open-pollinated plant is an heirloom. So to be an heirloom really is a mix of things.

Are you thinking about diving into the world of heirlooms for the first time? Kathy's advice for beginners is to start small, preferably with something you like to eat, because many heirloom varieties are known for tasting better than their modern counterparts.

Kathy also recommends taking good notes. Write down what you grew, how well it did and what the growing conditions were like. The following year, take a look at the results and make changes as needed. Nothing is worse than discovering the best tomato you've ever had only to realize you forgot the variety's name.

Not into veggies? Heirloom seeds are out there for flower and herb gardeners, too. Baker Creek has a huge selection of heirloom flower seeds available for purchase both on its site, *rareseeds.com*, and in its catalog.

Some are true antiques. The purplish-black Nigra hollyhock, for instance, was planted by Thomas Jefferson at Monticello and was mentioned by an earlier grower in 1629.

Though these historic flowers and herbs have disappeared faster than heirloom vegetables, they still exist, ready to wow you with the beauty and fragrance that charmed our ancestors.

If you aren't yet convinced that heirlooms are for you, sample some at a farmers market. Chances are, you'll be a fan. We hear the watermelon is to die for!

top heirloom picks

Jere Gettle, co-founder of Baker Creek Heirloom Seeds and pictured below with his family, shares his favorite heirloom varieties with us. Give them a try!

Beans

Jere recommends beans to any newbie. Nothing's easier to grow.

JERE'S FAVORITES: Chinese Red Noodle, Purple Podded Pole (above), Roma II

GROWING TIPS: Grow in full sun. Climbing types will need the support of a trellis or fence.

WHY WE LOVE THEM: Beans are packed with vital nutrients, and there's no limit to the ways you can use them in the kitchen.

Jere and his wife, Emilee, wrote *The Heirloom Life Gardener* with Meghan Sutherland. Along with growing tips, it features veggie profiles and a rundown of the benefits of locally grown food.

Carrots

Why stop at orange ones when you can have purple, red, white or yellow? Remember that the bolder the carrot's color, the more nutrients it has.

JERE'S FAVORITES: Chantenay Red Core, Little Fingers, Parisienne

GROWING TIPS: In most areas, carrots should be planted in spring or fall. Northern gardeners can store them right in the garden by covering the roots with straw or leaves right after the ground lightly freezes.

WHY WE LOVE THEM: They're so versatile! Carrots are delicious raw, or cooked in soups and stews.

Cucumbers

Try heirloom cucumbers in green, white and even orange.

JERE'S FAVORITES: Lemon Cuke, Japanese Long, Dragon's Egg (below)

GROWING TIPS: Sow seeds directly into soil. A trellis will make cucumbers a lot easier to harvest. They thrive in full sun.

WHY WE LOVE THEM: There's nothing like a fresh, crunchy cuke straight from the garden. Or go the Asian route and try steaming or stir-frying them.

Eggplant

Eggplant is fairly easy to grow. There are hundreds of varieties out there in almost every color imaginable.

JERE'S FAVORITES: Little Green, Rosa Bianca, Fengyuan Purple

GROWING TIPS: Indoors, grow eggplant from seed in pots about 10 weeks before winter's last frost. Harvest when the fruit is glossy and firm to the touch.

WHY WE LOVE IT: Low in calories and full of nutrients, it can be used as a meat substitute in lots of dishes, so it's perfect for vegetarians.

Lettuce

As a rule of thumb, the darker the lettuce leaf, the bigger the nutritional punch it packs.

JERE'S FAVORITES: Little Gem, Red Romaine, Forellenschluss

GROWING TIPS: Lettuce will grow in most garden soils. In cool areas, you can grow it through the summer; gardeners in warm climates can harvest lettuce throughout winter.

WHY WE LOVE IT: For salads and sandwiches, lettuce is a must. Many Chinese dishes use steamed lettuce. If you're feeling brave, give it a shot.

Melons

Some varieties can be grown in as few as 65 days. But if you're not in a hurry, you have thousands more to choose from.

JERE'S FAVORITES: Old Time Tennessee, Banana, Charentais

GROWING TIPS: Melons thrive in warm, dry areas but need additional care in other climates. Knowing when they're ripe can be tricky; watch for the fruit to change color and soften a bit.

WHY WE LOVE THEM: You can't beat that sweet taste, and the huge number of varieties means there's at least one that suits every gardener.

Onions

These flavorful bulbs were among the first things the Pilgrims planted in the New World. Any good cook knows why.

JERE'S FAVORITES: Red of Florence, Flat of Italy (below), Australian Brown

GROWING TIPS: Generally speaking, you'll want to look for so-called short-day onions in the South and long-day onions in the North.

WHY WE LOVE THEM: Raw, sauteed or deep-fried—onions add a flavor that nothing else can match.

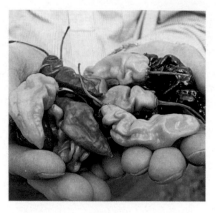

Peas

Most pea varieties are bright green, but you can find snow peas with yellow and purplish-blue pods.

JERE'S FAVORITES: Golden Sweet Snow, Little Marvel, Oregon Sugar Pod II (above)

GROWING TIPS: Most varieties are climbers, so use a trellis or other support system. Garden pea pods are ready to be harvested when they're plump and bright green. You can harvest edible podded peas before the seeds swell.

WHY WE LOVE THEM: Packed with vitamins, protein and fiber, yummy pea pods brighten any meal.

Peppers

They're easy to grow, have a wide variety of flavor profiles, and are a rewarding veggie for beginners to try out in the garden.

JERE'S FAVORITES: Melrose, Orange Bell, all the Marconi peppers in a variety of colors

GROWING TIPS: Try using raised beds. Peppers love warm soil, good drainage and lots of sunshine.

WHY WE LOVE THEM: The options are infinite. It's fun to experiment with color, size and degree of spiciness, from mild bell peppers to sizzling chilies.

Radishes

There are two types: Small salad radishes are commonly eaten raw, while winter radishes are much larger and are good for cooking.

JERE'S FAVORITES: Round Spanish Black, Chinese Red Meat, Chinese Green Luobo (Qingluobo)

GROWING TIPS: Radishes need a lot of organic matter for good drainage. Plant seeds in full sun, about a quarter-inch deep.

WHY WE LOVE THEM: Small radishes add crunch to cold foods. To perk up a stir-fry, try radish greens.

Squash

Don't let the strange appearance of some squashes turn you off. Experimenting with these prolific growers will bring lots of rewards.

JERE'S FAVORITES: Gelber Englischer Custard, Sucrine Du Berry, Yokohama

GROWING TIPS: Grow squash in rich soil with plenty of drainage and in full sun.

WHY WE LOVE THEM: Any seeds you don't save for planting can be eaten. Soak overnight in salt water and then roast them in the oven.

seed savers exchange

Seed Savers Exchange is a nonprofit organization making huge strides to preserve heirlooms by maintaining a network of gardeners committed to saving and sharing seeds and plants. SSE's assistant curator, Jenna Sicuranza, is pictured above with a bounty of squash varieties.

Exchange members receive a 10 percent discount on purchases from the SSE catalog and get exclusive publications throughout the year. For more information about the organization or to become a member, visit SSE's website, *seedsavers.org*. Not a member? That's no problem. Anyone can order from the catalog, so check out the site and buy your first heirloom!

dry your own herbs

Got an abundance of herbs in the garden? Dry and store them for cooking and flavored oils. A bonus? They make fabulous gifts!

STEP 1. Gather the fresh herbs from the garden, preferably in the morning after the dew has dried but before the heat of the sun has had a chance to wilt the leaves.

STEP 2. Spread out the leaves on a clean surface or tie them into loose bundles and hang to dry. This will take several days. If you're impatient or need them right away, you can nuke them in the microwave. Start out at 1 minute, check for dryness, and continue at 30-second increments until the leaves are dry and crisp.

STEP 3. Strip the leaves from the tough stems.

STEP 4. Working with one herb at a time, crush the leaves into pieces of the desired size and store in airtight jars in a cool, dark place for maximum freshness.

STEP 5. If you prefer ground herbs, you can whir the dried herbs in a clean electric coffee grinder. Pack the grinder as full as you can get it. Grind until the leaves are reduced to the desired fineness. It helps to hold the grinder and shake it a little as it grinds.

STEP 6. If there are tough bits of stem remaining, sift the herbs through a fine sieve to remove them. Put the herbs in a jar or canister until you're ready to use them.

Project courtesy of *Little House in the Suburbs* by Deanna Caswell and Daisy Siskin. For more information, visit *betterwaybooks.com*.

use dried herbs to make flavored oils

- Place the dried herbs into dry, sterilized bottles.

- Warm olive oil below a simmer (don't boil it) just until you can see some movement in the pan, but no bubbles. While the oil is hot, use a funnel to pour it into the bottles over the herbs.

- When the oil is cool, cap it and let it sit for a minimum of two weeks to allow it to absorb the flavors of the herbs. Pour it through a strainer into new sterilized bottles, removing the steeped herb. If you like, add a sprig or two of a dried herb or a few peppercorns to the new bottles for visual interest.

- Keep in a cool, dark place and use within a couple of months.

1

garden herbs

These fragrant, delicious herbs add flavor to any kitchen concoction.

BY DANIELLE CALKINS

Smell that? The fragrance in my kitchen is absolutely divine. Snippets of fresh basil are mingling with my pasta sauce. And me? I'm in heaven. If you crave seductive scents like this all year long, growing fresh herbs will do the trick. Whether you're tilling a full vegetable garden out back or tending a few small containers in your kitchen, you'll find success by picking the right plants for your space.

The minute I got my hands on Andrea Bellamy's *Sugar Snaps and Strawberries*, I was hooked. Yes, I adore the book's title, but, even better, I found all the growing tips I needed for planting my favorite herbs this season. Last summer I grew basil and oregano—and I'm ready to branch out. That will mean even more flavorful meals from my kitchen.

These Top 10 herbs not only are wonderful to sniff and taste, they'll save you time and money when you plan menus. Best of all, many can be dried for use all year long. Look for them from our friends at Bonnie Plants. With so many herb varieties to choose from, you'll find just the right ones to add tempting aromas to your own home.

1 Apple Mint

(*Mentha suaveolens*, Zones 5 to 9)
One of the easiest herbs to grow, apple mint is a natural for containers or other small spaces. While you'll enjoy the mint flavor, the unexpected fruity tones are delightful, too. Be sure to keep up with the wandering ways of this herb and pick leaves frequently. With container plants, tucking stray mint back into the pot will help control growth.
TASTES GREAT IN: Two things to try: Add crushed leaves to ice water for a refreshing summer drink, or steep in hot water for tea.

2 Chive

(*Allium* spp., Zones 3 to 9)
Versatile chives impart a subtle oniony flavor to food. Deadhead or grow in containers to keep these plants in check. With their mauve flowers, chives are pretty as edging plants for beds and filler plants for containers. Harvest from spring through fall.
TASTES GREAT IN: For a tasty side dish, add chives to all kinds of vegetables—simply saute in oil along with some garlic. Or impress your guests by topping a salad with some chive blossoms.

5 Oregano

(*Origanum* spp., Zones 5 to 10)
Though it's similar to marjoram, frost-tolerant oregano is a safer choice for cold climates—and here in Wisconsin, winter can go beyond cold to brutal. Drying oregano increases its flavor. Simply cut whole stems, hang them in a cool, dry place, and *voilà*—a lovely herb to sprinkle on pizza and much more any month of the year.
TASTES GREAT IN: Skip the Mediterranean restaurant tonight and make a savory frittata instead. Adding fresh oregano will provide just the right touch to inspire you to eat at home more often.

6 Dill

(*Anethum graveolens*, annual)
While dill grows well in the garden alongside tomatoes, sweet peppers or chilies, it needs space to flourish. It wasn't until dill arrived in my CSA box last year as part of my crop share that I first had the chance to use it. Since it's easy to grow in full sun, I'll try planting my own this time around. I've been warned it likes to self-sow, so keep that in mind.
TASTES GREAT IN: Calling all pickle fans! Summer is the perfect time to make your own fresh, delicious dills. When it's warm out, I could polish off a jar of these crunchy treats pretty quickly all by myself.

9 Parsley

(*Petroselinum crispum*, annual)
Let's first distinguish between two popular parsley varieties. If cooking is your calling, flat-leafed Italian parsley has your name on it; it's delicious in dozens of dishes. Looking for an attractive container plant to use as a garnish? Curly-leafed parsley is the way to go. Both varieties are relatively straightforward to grow.
TASTES GREAT IN: Grab your calendar and make note of summer cookouts and tailgating parties. When a potato or veggie salad is your dish to pass, you'll be grateful for the fresh green sprigs and leaves from your parsley plant.

10 Sage

(*Salvia officinalis*, Zones 5 to 9)
Here's a champion herb if you ever saw one, a species that works equally well in borders, beds and containers. The gray-green, chartreuse or dusky-purple foliage is an eye-catching accent to any planting. After four years, the plant becomes woody and may need to be replaced. And that's easy to do: Just take a cutting and start a new plant.
TASTES GREAT IN: While many of us add sage to turkey or chicken stuffing around the winter holidays, it's also an enchanting seasoning for couscous, quinoa and other pastas and grains.

3
Basil
(*Ocimum* spp., annual)

A favorite in Asian and Italian cooking, basil grows marvelously in containers. Basil seeds can begin indoors four to six weeks before the last frost. To harvest, pinch off the tips of the stems; do this regularly for best growth. At the end of the season, freeze or dry what's left.

TASTES GREAT IN: While basil is delicious in almost any Italian dish, don't be afraid to take another tack. For a simple vinaigrette or marinade, heat white wine vinegar and pour over fresh basil. After 24 hours, strain and discard the leaves.

4
Rosemary
(*Rosmarinus officinalis*, Zones 8 to 11)

If you're looking for an edible yet substantial shrub, rosemary will fit your yard beautifully. Grow it in containers or in the garden in milder regions, or you can even trim it as a hedge. For container planting, use pots at least 8 inches deep. In cool climates, overwinter rosemary indoors, but keep an eye out for powdery mildew.

TASTES GREAT IN: Add rosemary to any poultry dish and you'll have a crowd-pleaser. Use the edible flowers in salads, herb butters and cream cheese spreads.

7
Cilantro
(*Coriandrum sativum*, annual)

You may know this popular plant as coriander, a name it shares with the sweet spice made by drying the seeds. Cilantro plants, with their aromatic dark-green leaves, do well in both gardens and containers. The tiny white flowers attract beneficial insects, so try spreading these plants throughout your garden.

TASTES GREAT IN: Cilantro leaves are a must in Mexican cooking and many Asian cuisines. Try fiesta grilled corn or cilantro potatoes for dinner tonight. Sounds good to me!

8
Thyme
(*Thymus* spp., Zones 5 to 9)

Adorned with pretty purple, pink or white flowers, this silvery herb likes containers that are at least 6 inches deep. Avoid overwatering and be sure to pinch back the tips to encourage bushy growth, or simply snip entire stems at soil level. As long as you avoid overwatering, thyme will thrive in full sun and well-drained soil.

TASTES GREAT IN: Thyme is superb with sweet corn; try adding a few leaves to the butter before slathering it on a freshly grilled ear. I guarantee you'll love it.

start seeds and save

Joyce Cox of Easton, Maryland, found that milk shake cups are perfect for starting seeds. She saves them until late winter or spring, when she punches a few holes in the bottoms, puts a little soil inside, plants the seeds and adds water. She then puts plastic wrap across the openings and adds the lids.

This creates a greenhouse effect, giving the seeds ample warmth and moisture to sprout. When sprouts reach the top, she just removes the lids, and the plants keep growing.

Take a little inspiration from Joyce and try starting your seeds in recycled vessels this spring. Here are a few more ideas:

Strawberry containers   Yogurt containers
Milk cartons   Egg cartons
Oatmeal boxes

make a
hula hoop plant cover

Keep precious plants cozy with this clever hula hoop cover, which will give you warmer soil for earlier planting. Best of all, the colorful frame will look cheerful all year round.

STEP 1. Insert the lengths of bamboo cane into the ends of the four hula hoop sections so that half of a bamboo cane is sticking out from each end of the hoops.

STEP 2. Push the bamboo part of the hoop structure into the earth on either side of the crops that need protection or the seeds and soil that you would like to keep warm.

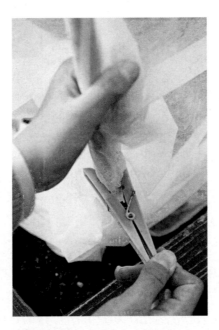

STEP 3. Cover the hula hoops with the piece of horticultural fleece. This is a much easier job if there are two of you.

STEP 4. Secure the fleece at the bottom of each of the hoops with a clothespin. Make sure you gather up the fleece before attaching it so there are no gaps to let in cold air.

supplies

- 2 hula hoops (cut in half)
- 8 pieces of bamboo cane, each 18 in. long
- 6 ft. of horticultural fleece
- 8 large colored clothespins

TRY THIS IN SUMMER. Take off the horticultural fleece and use your cloche frame as a colorful support for growing dwarf climbing beans or pea plants.

Project courtesy of *Garden Crafts for Children* by Dawn Isaac from CICO Books. It's available for $19.95 at *cicobooks.com.*

You can save time and money by just planning ahead.

BY NOELLE JOHNSON

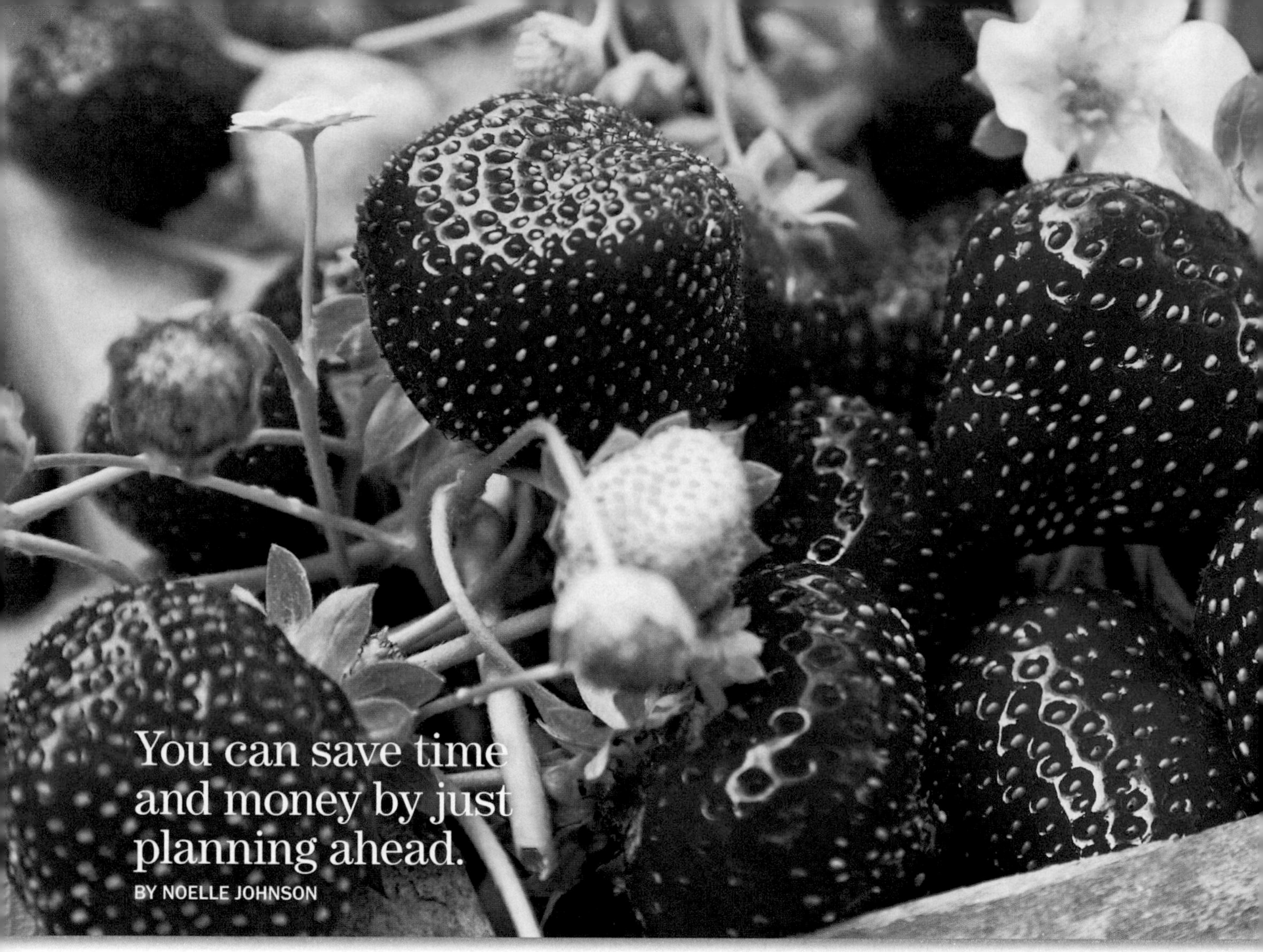

companion

Having a beautiful, healthy garden is a goal that many of us work hard to achieve. But did you know that certain plants are able to do much of the work for you?

It's called companion gardening, and people have been practicing it for centuries. It's simple, really—companion plants are those with qualities that benefit other plants. It's true that not all horticulturists agree with these backyard home remedies, but many gardeners have used them for years to repel damaging insects, add nutrients to the soil, improve the growth of vegetables and prevent plant disease. Is it worth a try? You decide.

gardening

The practice of pairing plants isn't new. Native Americans used the "three sisters" method, growing beans, corn and squash together. The corn provided support for the beans, the squash shaded the soil and kept weeds down, and the beans replenished the soil with nitrogen at the end of the season. Now that's a mutually beneficial relationship!

When it comes to companion plants, some pairings aren't always obvious. For example, who would think that strawberries would love being planted next to onions, or that roses enjoy being surrounded by garlic? Yet both combinations work well.

Natural Insect Repellent

Using plants with insect-repelling qualities is an easy way to decrease the use of insecticides and still reduce insect damage. The scents of basil, catnip, garlic, marigold and petunia repel some damaging insects without harming beneficial ones. There's still a debate among scientists, and results may vary from one garden to the next, but you may want to give it a try. You've got nothing to lose and some possible benefits to gain.

Another way to keep damaging insects away from your garden is to trick them by masking the other plants' scents. You can easily do this by mixing fragrant herbs like basil, chives, oregano, rosemary and sage with your other plants. Because the strong-smelling herbs cover up the scents of plants that attract, damaging insects often will leave them alone.

Certain plants act as magnets for bad bugs. Geraniums, lantana, petunias and nasturtiums are irresistible to many insects. For instance, whiteflies love lantana, and aphids can't resist nasturtiums, so those pests may focus on their favorites, rather than feasting on your other plants. This method is definitely worth a shot. Try interspersing these magnet plants throughout your garden and, though it's not a guaranteed solution, see if that does the trick. Keep monitoring your plants and address the problem early.

Good Bugs and No-Fuss Fertilizer

Next, consider plants that will attract more good bugs. Since they naturally help keep bad bugs away from your garden, they're a perfect fit for companion gardening. Flowering plants such as alyssum, bachelor's button, bee balm and cosmos not only lure helpful insects that will prey upon damaging insects, but also attract pollinators such as bees.

One of the easiest ways to draw in beneficial insects is to include plants with the bell-shaped flowers that often appeal to them. Foxglove, Canterbury bells and campanula are all good options. Plants in the dill family will also bring in good bugs that will eat pests. As a bonus, dill is also a host for swallowtails.

With companion planting, you can save money on fertilizer, too. Most plants enjoy enriched, fertile soil. But instead of adding fertilizer, why not let plants do the work for you?

Alfalfa, beans, beets, clover and kohlrabi all add nutrients to the soil when they die at the end of their growing season. Alfalfa, beans and clover take nitrogen from the air and convert it into a form of the element that plants can absorb through the soil. Beets and kohlrabi naturally add vital minerals to the earth.

Benefits to Veggies

Many gardeners believe complementary plants in the vegetable garden can boost growth and flavor because they secrete substances into the soil that help other vegetables. To improve the flavor of your tomatoes, for example, plant basil alongside them. Or try planting chamomile with

DUAL BENEFITS. Bell-shaped flowers are naturally good options for luring good insects into your yard. This foxglove (left) is attracting a bee, which will help keep the entire garden pollinated. Beans (center) add nutrients to the soil at the end of the growing season, while sunflowers (right) offer welcome afternoon shade to other plants on sunny days.

cabbage, cucumbers or onions to improve their flavor and make them grow faster.

In addition to repelling damaging insects, herbs such as basil, garlic, mint, sage and thyme help reduce disease in your garden. Onions provide similar benefits, and they also prevent mold on strawberries.

Tall Shadows

Another easy form of companion gardening is simply to use tall plants. They provide shade to sun-sensitive plants, and also act as a windbreak. Sunflowers planted next to your vegetable garden, for example, can protect cucumbers and tomatoes from the searing afternoon sun.

With all the benefits that companion plants offer your garden, why would you spend extra time spraying for pests and fertilizing? Just choose the right pairings and I believe you could enjoy a thriving natural garden full of bigger, tastier, healthier plants—with a minimal amount of effort.

FOXGLOVE, MIKE POWLES / OXFORD SCIENTIFIC / GETTY IMAGES; BEANS, GAP PHOTOS / ELKE BORKOWSKI; SUNFLOWER, PETE TURNER / GETTY IMAGES; CONTAINER, BURPEE HOME GARDENS

strawberry salad bowl

Mixed containers of flowers, herbs, fruits and vegetables are a hot new trend. This season, experiment with using both flowers and edible plants, then reap the rewards in the kitchen.

Here's a fabulous container recipe to get you started. The mixture of strawberries and lettuce not only looks good, it will make a super salad, too. Make the container extra fun by using an old colander the way Burpee Home Gardens did. Plant the combination in a 14-inch container and place it in full sun.

A Gourmet Blend lettuce (1)
B Heatwave Blend lettuce (1)
C Little Caesar lettuce (1)
D Berri Basket Pink Strawberry (2)

Learn how to select (and grow) some of the best new apples on the market.

time for
apples

BY KEN WYSOCKY

When autumn rolls around, it never fails to evoke memories of the days when I used to take my daughters to pick apples at local orchards in southeastern Wisconsin.

To me, autumn and apples are partners on par with Halloween and pumpkins—you just can't imagine one without the other. Crisp as a sunny October afternoon and painted in hues that mirror fall's vibrant red and yellow foliage, apples are the quintessential autumnal fruit.

APPLE-PLANTING TIP

Plant your apple tree where it will receive early-morning sun and enjoy good air circulation. This reduces the risk of your trees suffering from powdery mildew and other diseases.

APPLE-PICKING AND STORAGE TIPS

- Look for fully colored fruits that are firm and free of bruises.

- If the stems consistently remain on the tree when you pull off apples, instead of coming off with them, the fruits aren't yet ripe enough for picking.

- Store apples in a refrigerator or a cool place that's between 34 and 40 degrees. Some varieties keep better than others; the best ones will easily keep up to 90 days.

- Note that the fruits on the outside edge of the tree's canopy ripen first.

Because they keep so well, we enjoy apples year-round. And enjoy we do—we each consume more than 19 pounds of apples a year, according to the Agriculture Council of America. That popularity extends around the globe, as apple trees are the most widely grown deciduous fruit trees worldwide.

Try Growing Your Own

Apples have been a mainstay in American diets since the Pilgrims planted apple trees nearly 400 years ago. In fact, the saying "An apple a day keeps the doctor away" is more than just a folksy adage. Apples are fat-, sodium- and cholesterol-free, contain only minimal calories and are a good source of potassium, folic acid and vitamin C.

Another interesting apple-related fact: You can plant your own trees and become a pomologist, a cultivator of fruit trees. But before buying, perform a taste test and see which varieties you enjoy the most.

You have plenty to choose from, as more than 2,500 varieties are grown in the United States alone! However, keep in mind that apple trees don't do as well in warmer climates, because they require a winter chill to produce fruit.

Apple trees fall into three groups: dwarf, semidwarf (12 to 16 feet tall) or standard (15 to 40 feet tall) varieties. Dwarf varieties are popular because they fit in any size landscape and bear fruit several years sooner than the standard varieties (usually three to four years for dwarf and five to seven years for standard).

Can't Plant Just One

Most apple trees are grafted onto a hardy rootstock, with a bud or shoot (known as a "scion") of the desired apple variety grafted to a hardy, sometimes dwarfing, root system. When shopping, keep in mind that a younger tree will adapt readily to transplant, speeding up its establishment.

Unless you already have an apple or crabapple tree in your yard, you'll need to buy two different varieties of trees. Why? Most apple trees don't self-pollinate. And those cultivars that do self-pollinate, such as Gala, Golden Delicious, Granny Smith and Jonathan, will bear much more fruit if cross-pollinated.

Also keep in mind that some varieties aren't compatible with others, while others—such as Jonagold, Winesap and Northern Spy—are sterile. They produce best when cross-pollinated, but their pollen won't pollinate other apple trees. Consult your local nursery or county extension office for more information.

Select varieties whose bloom times overlap and that are hardy in your planting zone. Furthermore, don't use insecticides when the trees are blooming, as bees are essential to cross-pollination.

Some apple varieties are more disease-resistant than others; for example, Pristine is resistant to scab, fire blight, powdery mildew and cedar apple rust. Again, a local nursery or county extension office can help you find trees best suited for your area.

APPLE-PRUNING TIP

Prune apple trees when dormant, preferably late winter or early spring before growth begins. Pruning encourages air circulation and light penetration, which reduce disease and increase fruit production.

a new apple a day

Think beyond Red Delicious and give these less familiar varieties a try.

SWEETANGO. It's a cross between the popular Honeycrisp and Zestar! varieties. The apple is crisp and juicy, excellent for eating raw.

JONAGOLD. As its name implies, pairing Jonathan and Golden Delicious varieties created this yellow-green favorite with a red-orange blush. It's good for snacking and cooking.

HONEYCRISP. If you haven't tried one yet, make this the year. Exceptionally crisp, juicy and sweet, it is ideal for baking and stores extremely well.

CAMEO. This hearty, juicy apple has deep flavor and crunchy texture—a perfect choice for eating out of hand.

AUTUMN GLORY. A cross between Fuji and Golden Delicious, this variety is sweet and firm and—surprise!—has a subtle cinnamon flavor.

JAZZ. A tangy-sweet cross between Royal Gala and Braeburn, this one's equally delightful for eating and cooking.

PINATA. Dubbed "the foodies' apple," it's a cross of three varieties, including Golden Delicious. The extra-juicy, thin-skinned fruit is delicious raw, roasted or in a pie.

Let's Start Digging

Spring is the best time to plant apple trees. They do best in full sun and don't like "wet feet," so well-draining soil is a must. To maximize cross-pollination, don't plant dwarf trees more than 20 feet apart, semidwarfs beyond 50 feet apart or standard species more than 100 feet apart.

Dig a hole at least twice the width of and at the same depth as the root-ball. Fill in the planting hole with existing soil. Using different, looser dirt discourages the roots from extending beyond the planting hole to the surrounding soil.

When planting, be sure the "bud union," where the scion meets the rootstock, is 2 to 3 inches above ground level. Water and gently tamp the soil as you replace the dirt around the root-ball to remove air pockets.

Surround the tree with a cylinder of hardware cloth at least 4 feet high and several inches into the soil. This will keep critters out. Unless it is a bare-root or top-heavy tree, staking isn't recommended.

As your tree grows, prune branches to shape the tree. It's also helpful to thin out small fruits when they finally appear. Fruits generally grow in clusters; thin them down to one fruit per cluster (the largest or healthiest-looking one) when they're about as big as a grape, and keep the fruits 4 to 6 inches apart. This will help the apples grow larger and reduce the chances of limbs snapping under the fruits' weight.

It may seem like a while before your tree produces fruit. But when it does, I guarantee this prolific tree will be the apple of your eye.

TEPEE PLANTING TIPS

Unlike bush beans, pole beans can grow as tall as 8 feet and will benefit greatly from a tepee-style structure to climb. If the poles of your tepee are farther apart than the structure featured here, fill the spaces with a zigzag pattern of twine to provide additional climbing surfaces. When planting the seeds, space them about 2 inches apart around the perimeter of the tepee. As the vines mature, train them to climb the poles, and mulch with straw or grass clippings to help retain soil moisture.

build a
thrifty garden tower

For climbing plants like garden peas and green beans, you can't beat this tepee-style support for simplicity and portability. The bamboo poles make it relatively lightweight.

STEP 1. Choose a location for the tower in your garden.

STEP 2. Bundle the bamboo together and wrap the rubber band around the top of the bundle. Spread the bottom of the bundle to create the perimeter of a tepee, with the poles spaced equally apart.

STEP 3. Hammer the gutter spikes into the ground around the perimeter, each one perpendicular to the end of a pole.

STEP 4. Tie or wire the bamboo to the spikes to secure the structure to the ground.

STEP 5. Reinforce the rubber band at the top of the tepee with rope or wire.

supplies

- Ten ½-in. bamboo poles, 6 ft. each
- Strong rubber band
- Hammer
- 10 gutter spikes
- ¼-in.-thick rope or wire
- Utility knife or wire cutter

Project courtesy of *The Vegetable Gardener's Book of Building Projects*, by the editors at Storey Publishing. For more information, go to *storey.com*.

1

tropical favorites

With a sunny window and a little patience, you can grow your own.

BY STACY TORNIO

If you're a gardener who enjoys a challenge, it's time to go tropical! Laurelynn and Byron Martin, co-owners of Logee's Plants for Home & Garden in Danielson, Connecticut, and authors of the book *Growing Tasty Tropical Plants*, have been helping people grow oranges, lemons, dragon fruit and more in their homes for years.

You might think these fruits thrive only in mild, sunny climates. But with the increasing number of ornamentals and dwarf varieties on the market, it's easier than ever to grow your favorite exotic fruit.

We're profiling some of our top choices from Laurelynn and Byron's book here, but you can pick up a copy for yourself to get more inspiration. With sunlight and the right container, you'll have a whole new take on what a houseplant can be.

1
Lemon
(Citrus limon)

If you're just getting into tropical plants, lemons are a good place to start. They grow 3 to 5 feet, but you can also grow them in a hanging basket. Use the fruits as they ripen, or leave them on the tree to harvest throughout the year.
WHY WE LOVE IT: It's easy! The Meyer cultivar is one of the most popular; its fruits produce almost twice as much juice as ordinary lemons. Ponderosa is also a good option, because it bears fruit easily.

2
Black pepper
(Piper nigrum)

Yes, you can grow your own spices, too. Pepper is a natural for containers. After a few years in a pot, one plant will produce an abundance of peppercorns. The woody vine grows 2 to 3 feet tall with support and pruning.
WHY WE LOVE IT: Black peppers fruit most of the year, stopping for only a month or two in winter when light levels are low.

5
Dragon fruit
(Hylocereus undatus)

Not only does it have spectacular large fruits, it perfumes the air with fragrant nighttime blossoms. Dragon fruit grows 4 to 6 feet on sprawling vines, so you'll need a pot trellis to hold it up. If you grow it indoors, move it outside in spring so it can bloom in summer and then fruit in fall. The inside of the fruit is soft and sweet, like a cross between a pear and kiwi.
WHY WE LOVE IT: The scales on dragon fruit, which give the plant its name, are a sight to behold. Keep in mind that when it flowers, you will need to hand-pollinate.

6
Myrtle-leaf orange
(Citrus myrtifolia)

One of the most popular ornamental fruits, this compact plant, growing 2 to 4 feet high, fits nicely on a windowsill. Give it lots of sunlight and keep it on the dry side to avoid root rot. Myrtle-leaf oranges are a bit sour, but they'll stay on the branch for months.
WHY WE LOVE IT: Its tight growth habit makes it perfect for bonsai culture. You can keep it in a small container for years.

9
Banana
(Musa spp.)

As the Martins write, "Growing your own bananas in a pot is always a conversation starter, but harvesting the small bananas is even more impressive." The plants have a distinctly tropical look, growing 3 to 6 feet tall with large leaves. Make sure you give banana plants enough food, water and sunlight for best results.
WHY WE LOVE IT: It's so much fun to pick your own bananas! Good cultivars to try include Dwarf Lady Finger, with small, finger-sized bananas, or Vente Cohol, the earliest-fruiting banana.

10
Dwarf pomegranate
(Punica granatum)

Nana is the cultivar you'll want to buy. Most pomegranates need winter dormancy with chilling temperatures to promote bud formation, but this one doesn't, making it a prime choice for indoor culture. It grows 1 to 3 feet in a pot, so it's small enough to display on a large windowsill. The tart, 1- to 2-inch fruits ripen from green to red.
WHY WE LOVE IT: It'll tolerate dry soil and air, so you don't have to worry about watering it all the time, though you shouldn't let it wilt. The size makes it ideal for small spaces.

3 Pineapple
(Ananus comosus)

This is one of the most fun tropical plants to grow, but you'll need a little patience. It takes two years for a pineapple to start producing fruit, and along the way it will need lots of heat and direct sunlight. The plant will grow 2 to 3 feet and can bloom or fruit anytime throughout the year.

WHY WE LOVE IT: What's not to love? Pineapple is sweet and juicy—and it just looks cool to have one growing in your house. Look for cultivars such as Royale or Smooth Cayenne for best results.

4 Star fruit
(Averrhoa carambola)

Slice one in half and you'll see a five-pointed star that's up to 4 inches across—the whole fruit is 7 inches long. In the tropics, trees grow up to 30 feet tall, and one has been known to feed an entire village. Indoors, it grows up to 5 feet with pruning.

WHY WE LOVE IT: The sweet fruit's shape alone is enough to make it a must-have. As a bonus, it's loaded with good-for-you antioxidants and flavonoids.

7 Passion fruit
(Passiflora spp.)

You've probably heard of passionflower vine, with its gorgeous tropical blooms, but did you know these vines produce fruit as well? Most varieties need cross-pollination to fruit, so indoor plants will require hand-pollination. This woody vine grows 3 to 6 feet with support. The fruit is tart, light and tangy.

WHY WE LOVE IT: The blooms before the fruit are stunning! Each flower lasts only for a day, but they're worth it.

8 Avocado
(Persea americana)

If you want to grow these emerald beauties, avoid the temptation of starting your own from an avocado pit. While it's a fun experiment, the plants hardly ever fruit. Instead, invest in a tree, which will grow to be 3 to 6 feet tall. The fruits need up to six months to ripen, so be patient!

WHY WE LOVE IT: It's a handsome ornamental plant, with glossy leaves and attractive fruit. The Day cultivar is by far the easiest to grow in a small pot.

amazing edibles

This is just the tip of the iceberg! *Growing Tasty Tropical Plants* offers dozens of other suggestions to try indoors. Here are a few you'll find in the book:

Grapefruit	**Coffee**
Cinnamon	**Tea**
Guava	**Chocolate**
Tangerine	**Citron**
Papaya	**Lime**
Olive	**Kumquat**

garden Projects

Beautify your backyard with easy, money-saving projects for gardeners of all ages. Bring four-season interest to any landscape using pretty pots, unexpected plant combos and more. Make over your garden in no time.

RDA MKE

GARDEN
in a weekend

Give your garden a new look with five fresh ideas.

BY CRYSTAL RENNICKE

INSTEAD OF A VEGGIE GARDEN, TRY…
an edible landscape.

More than half of consumers—53 percent, according to research by the Garden Writers Association—grow vegetables, spending more money on edibles than annuals, perennials, trees and shrubs. But instead of confining the veggie garden to an out-of-the-way section of the backyard, they're looking for practical ways to include edibles throughout the landscape.

"Edible landscaping has been a growing trend in the last couple of years as a response to the economic recession," says Scott Mozingo of Burpee Home Gardens. "Growing vegetables is economical, safe and healthy, and gardeners are finding out that you don't need a large veggie garden to enjoy the benefits of growing edibles."

Many plant suppliers, including Burpee, now breed veggies to thrive in containers, beds and borders with other plants or flowers. Scott suggests that a cottage-style border filled with hardy, disease-resistant rose bushes, hydrangeas, zinnias and other cut flowers is an ideal spot for Blue Lake Bush beans or Sweet Heat peppers. Edge the bed with edible herbs such as parsley and thyme, and you've made a lush mini garden full of food, flowers and fragrance without sacrificing aesthetics or space. Other colorful varieties that work well in containers and other small spaces include Bright Lights Swiss chard, Boxwood basil and Pot Black eggplant.

A BITE TO EAT. You get the best of both worlds when you grow edibles like lettuce and strawberries among your blooms. Mix throughout the yard to truly integrate.

MAKEOVERS

Does your winter-weary garden need a little renovation this spring? Boost its appeal with these easy ideas based on traditional garden practices that have a modern twist. All of them can be completed in a single weekend, so get ready to roll up your sleeves. It's out with the old and in with the new!

INSTEAD OF ONE-NOTE CONTAINERS, TRY...
four-season combinations.

Gardeners love growing plants in containers, but most of us are tired of spending money on annuals year after year. To get the most from your containers, combine plants that will look good all year long. Choose a small shrub (try Blue Chip butterfly bush or Little Lime hydrangea) or a tree (Japanese maple or dwarf evergreens) with seasonal interest. Then add pretty perennials, spring bulbs, edibles or long-lasting annuals for a look that will last throughout the year.

Savvy growers can get more than one growing season out of containers by planting perennials, then moving them to the landscape at the end of the season. Other ideas for those in colder regions: Overwinter pots in an unheated garage, or bury them in the ground and insulate them with evergreen boughs and snow.

Perennials that tend to overwinter well in containers include lamium, coral bells, asters, clematis, hostas, coneflowers, bellflower, bugleweed and daylilies.

INSTEAD OF A POND, TRY…

Let's face it: Ponds are pretty, but they're also high-maintenance. Many gardeners would love a beautiful water feature in the yard, but a huge pond isn't practical for most of us.

You don't have to go all the way, though. To get the soothing sounds and tranquility of a water garden without the labor, more and more gardeners are incorporating small water features into their outdoor living spaces.

Garden centers report increased interest in tabletop water gardens, some of which retail for less than $100. Something as simple as a cut piece of stone or a beautiful glazed urn with bubbling water can beautify your backyard without the cost and effort of a pond.

You can DIY and make your own, too! All you need is a pump kit from your local garden center or hardware store. Be creative!

INSTEAD OF RAIN BARRELS, TRY…

a rain garden.

Responsible watering is increasingly popular, especially in dry areas. More gardeners are using rain barrels, but some are going a step further and creating their own rain gardens.

"Gardeners care about nature," says rain gardener Sue Ellingson of Madison, Wisconsin. "Stormwater runoff carries a lot of phosphorus and sediment to our lakes and streams. By creating a small rain garden in their yard, gardeners can make a big difference."

For her rain garden, Sue simply put a planting bed in the path of the rainwater running off her lot, but kept it away from the foundation of her house. She shaped a shallow depression to capture the runoff, filled the garden with native plants suited to her growing conditions, and that was it. Simple!

To try this yourself, check with your local Cooperative Extension office for a list of native plants that will work in a rain garden.

a small-scale water feature.

MAKE A SPLASH.
Once you get the hang of one mini backyard water feature, why not try grouping a few, as shown in the photo at left?

INSTEAD OF THE SAME OLD DECOR, TRY...

going color crazy.

Colorful outdoor accents are quick, easy ways to give your garden an updated look. New products in birding and gardening in bright hues and fun shades and designs add pizzazz, from bird feeders and containers to garden art, furniture, lighting and trellises.

Don't be shy about colorful flowers, either. Try massing flowers or leaves of one color throughout a bed (chartreuse looks beautiful filling out a shady area). Or just plant some of the season's hottest hues (purple and black are popular this year) where you need a little color.

A new coat of paint can go a long way, too. Try a bright or complementary color on your existing outdoor furniture, containers or garden structures to further accentuate your garden.

RECYCLING
in the garden

We love when people turn any kind of discarded objects into garden masterpieces. Take a look at these imaginative reader ideas.

1. Green Roof Makeover

This building near my town was used as part of the narrow-gauge railroad in the late 1800s. A few years ago, I fell in love with it and bought it, intending to use it for my small nursery. My husband was less than impressed, but he eventually came around and put his creativity to work. Then I had the idea of making the top of it a living roof. Everyone loves it, especially me!

KATHLEEN WHINNERY, *Lake City, Colorado*

2. Power of Paint

I'm always trying to think of ways to use items most people throw away. When my co-worker brought me her old satellite dish, I had my husband attach metal legs to the back so I could plant it in the ground. Then a friend painted this scene on it for me. It's been an unusual and pretty addition to our flower garden.

RUTH BUSCHJOST, *Jefferson City, Missouri*

3. Creative Corner

About 15 years ago, quite a few cinder blocks left over from a project were lying around my yard, creating a big eyesore. Then I had an idea. My daughters and I painted the blocks white, stacked them in tiers on top of planks around the corner of our house, filled them with soil, and planted perennials and annuals in them. We've been growing gorgeous flowers in our cinder blocks for years.

SHERI LOVE, *Forestville, New York*

4. Row, Row, Row Your Blooms

This is an old rowboat we've had in our garden for a long time. I filled it with impatiens that I grew from seed, so the entire thing was very inexpensive. We love going "Dumpster diving" to find other treasures like this to fill with plants.

GARY GEISTER, *Eagan, Minnesota*

DIY spoon rain chain

Make this rustic water feature for only a few dollars.

BY ALISON AUTH

Think gutters are ugly? Rain chains are a beautiful way to harness the power of water. The concept is simple: Surface tension and gravity guide the water down a chain. I decided to make a chain out of salvaged spoons. If you're looking for spoons at the thrift store, be sure to select thinner ones so they'll be easy to bend and drill, and choose a wire that is rustproof and easy to manipulate.

supplies

- **Spoons**
- **Wire**
- **Drill**
- **Sharp drill bit**
- **Needle-nose pliers**
- **Bench vise or clamp and pliers**

STEP 1. Decide how long you want the rain chain to be.

STEP 2. Using a bench vise, bend enough spoons to complete the project. If you don't have a vise, use a hand clamp to secure the flat part of the spoon against a table with the rest of it hanging over. Use pliers to bend the spoon down.

STEP 3. Remove the bowls from a dozen or so spoons. Use the same method as in Step 2, only bend each spoon back and forth until the bowl snaps off.

STEP 4. Drill holes in the end of each spoon handle, including the handles without bowls.

STEP 5. Put two spoons together back to back so the bowls are facing outward. Fit a bowl-less handle between the handles of the two spoons, leaving several inches extended past the spoons (see the top-right photo). The protruding end of the handle should have the hole in it. Wrap wire around all three handles just above the bowls. Then wire together the handles of the spoons at the other end as tightly as you can. Be sure to leave some extra wire for attaching the next segment. Repeat this step until you've used all your spoons.

STEP 6. Once all the segments are assembled, attach them to each other by twisting together the extra wire you left at both ends. Make sure to leave enough wire on the top end of your chain for hanging.

STEP 7. Hang the rain chain from a tree limb above a rain garden, or use it in place of a downspout above a splash block to direct water away from the house. You can also use a decorative glazed pot or rain barrel below the chain to collect water for use in the garden.

CARD

BOARD
gardening

Have a better garden in a few weeks with this easy, eco-friendly method. (Did we mention it's FREE, too?)

BY STACY TORNIO

I'm a bargain hunter. A penny-pincher. A cheapskate. Nothing makes me happier than finding thrifty and resourceful ways to save money on the things I need or want.

I'm also a gardener. And, as anyone who has ever tended a patch of tomatoes can attest, it's alarmingly easy to spend a lot of money on a garden. So you can imagine my excitement when I discovered a supercheap, supersimple way to have a better garden. Cardboard!

A couple of years ago, I heard that cardboard made a good foundation for new garden beds, so that fall I grabbed a few old boxes, flattened them over some grass in the backyard and waited. In spring, when it came time to plant, the cardboard had broken down and I had a lovely new garden bed of rich soil, ready for planting.

Something that's free and easy and makes for a better garden? I was hooked.

Now, I know my two green-thumbed—and thrifty—grandmothers would probably giggle if they heard me going on and on about this wonderful "new" decomposable method. After all, generations of gardeners have used paper and cardboard in one way or another. But what if cardboard is more than just mulch or a weed barrier? What if it's the key to a whole new approach to gardening—one that lets you spend less and use less while still getting excellent results?

A few brainstorming sessions later that involved both the *Birds & Blooms* staff and a team of experts, and we had a laundry list of ideas for our new approach. We call it cardboard gardening.

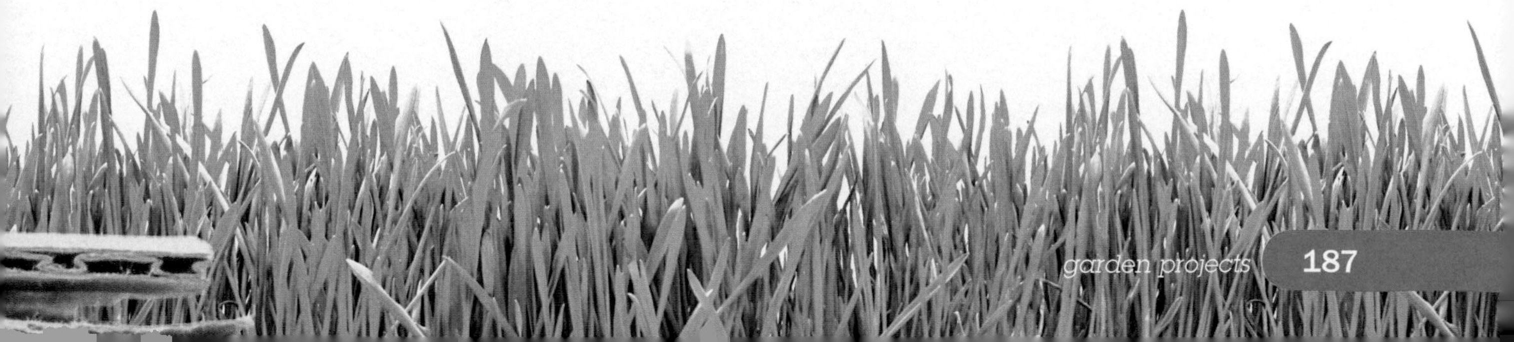

GET ON BOARD!

Be green and have great soil when you use it for …*compost*

When it comes to composting, you need a lot more brown matter (paper, leaves, sticks, etc.) than green (kitchen scraps). Essentially, you need a ratio of 25 to 1. Cardboard really comes in handy here—it's a composter's best friend!

Whether you have a compost pile or bin, cardboard is ideal brown material. Just break it down into manageable pieces and throw it in with the other stuff. As it decomposes, it will add nutrients your plants will love.

Try an innovative and new way to grow …*container gardens*

These days, the cost of container gardening can really add up. Save money and spend it on plants instead by using cardboard boxes as the containers. Treat them the way you'd treat conventional containers: Fill with soil, make sure you have proper drainage and don't forget to water.

But will a cardboard container really hold up for an entire season through watering, wind, rain and everything else you and nature throw at it? Along with a few other gardeners around the country, we tested some out, and the answer is—yes!

Sure, this approach might not be for those who like their spaces to look neat and tidy, but if you're adventurous, think *inside* the box here! Remember, with the right plants, by the end of summer you can't see the container anyway. If you'd like, add a little reinforcement with tape in any weak areas. Or line the box with a plastic bag with

SHARE WITH OTHERS. In addition to being an all-around good container, cardboard's handy for transplanting or dividing plants in spring and fall.

drainage holes to keep it from getting soggy. And if looks are important to you, try some of our ideas for dressing it up (keep reading!).

Think outside the box, and make some… *decorative containers*

They say you can't make a silk purse out of a sow's ear. But you really can make plain old cardboard look good, and it doesn't take much time, effort or money.

First the easy ideas: You can paint the box, wrap it in paper or cover it in old fabric. And if you're up for being a bit more creative, try some of our

other favorite materials: yarn, twine or rope.

My personal favorites are laminate and cork tiles. They're available with amazing designs these days, and you can pick them up at a home improvement store for just a few bucks. You'll probably need extra reinforcement for these, but they can transform a cardboard box into a container worthy of the front porch.

Say adios to unwanted grass when used as a… *weed barrier*

Cardboard, newspaper and other compostable material are quick and

look at cardboard in a new way!

dress it up!

There are dozens of materials you can use to camouflage cardboard. Here are a few of our favorites.

Rope
Yarn
Ceramic tiles
Corkboard
Duct tape
Ribbons
Paint
Leftover wallpaper
Sticks or twigs

Material scraps
Decorative plastic bags
Old curtains
Paper for decoupage
Sticks from ice cream bars
Wall or window clings
Wrapping paper
Laminate or vinyl

recycled sweatpants!

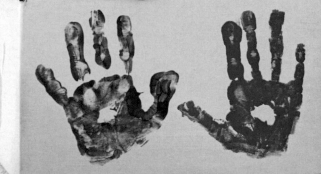

GET STARTED ON THE RIGHT TRACK...

BEFORE...

Inspect the cardboard and make sure it hasn't been contaminated with anything that might have been shipped in it. Also, if you plan to upcycle it into a container, reinforce any weak areas.

DURING...

If you're growing plants in the cardboard, water directly in the center to avoid drenching and weakening the sides. If using it as a mulch or weed barrier, keep it watered to aid in decomposition.

AFTER...

Leave the cardboard in the garden, letting it break down naturally. Or if you'd like, move it to your compost bin at the end of the season.

yes, it is as easy as it looks!

STEP BY STEP. Starting a new garden bed doesn't have to be hard. Just head for the recycling bin. We tested it out in our "backyard" at work last summer. In a couple of short months, we had a fresh bed, ready for plants.

easy fixes for weed problems. In just one growing season, you can reduce weeds by 75 percent or more.

Just place pieces of cardboard around the plants you want to protect. Water immediately to help the cardboard stay in place. (I say this because I've been that person chasing runaway cardboard caught by the wind.) You can add soil or mulch on top to reinforce it, too. The cardboard will suppress the weeds and eventually break down into the soil, adding useful organic matter.

Get foolproof results when starting
...new flower beds

The easiest way to start a brand-new garden bed is not with a tiller. Forget sweating behind heavy machinery, and use cardboard instead. That's how I first discovered the magic.

This method will take a bit longer, but it really is the simplest way to start a bed. Just outline the shape you want on your grass (try using a garden hose to form the template), use edging to keep the grass out, then cover the area with cardboard. Water immediately and top with soil, mulch, leaves or anything you have on hand to hold down the cardboard.

After a few months, you'll start to see the cardboard breaking down. Underneath, you'll find fresh garden soil, ready for plants. The best time to do this is in fall, so the cardboard can break down over the winter and you'll

1. FLATTEN CARDBOARD

be ready to go in spring. The prep work probably won't take much more than half an hour.

Lay the foundation for a fast and easy
...new pathway

Creating a new garden path might seem like a lot of work, but you can have a simple one in about an hour. No, this isn't a fancy-schmancy infomercial-type promise. All you need are cardboard, bricks or something else to outline the path, and mulch.

You're going to be placing the cardboard directly onto the grass or whatever other surface you're working on. Cardboard is thick enough so that you shouldn't have any stray grass or weeds poking up through it. (If you do, just pile on more cardboard.) Place the cardboard in the shape you want the path to take. Outline with bricks, then cover with soil and mulch. *Voilà*!

Jump-start your garden by using it for
...seed starters

The cost of seed-starting supplies can add up fast. Grow lights, special pots, fancy mats—I've tried them all.

CREATE A PATHWAY. A little cardboard and a lot of mulch go a long way. At right, we created a cardboard-based pathway in our test garden. It took just a couple of short hours, and then we were done!

2. PLACE DIRECTLY ONTO GRASS

3. PEEL IT BACK

4. ADD YOUR PLANTS

FRESH HERBS. For this windowsill planter, we first lined the box with plastic—this helps the cardboard hold up longer—and added drainage holes. Then we planted a few herbs and put 'em in a sunny window.

simply add a little sunshine

Cardboard boxes are the ideal solution for starting seeds because you can keep them growing inside longer, giving you stronger seedlings. (Don't forget to provide them with plenty of light for optimum results.) Then just plop the whole thing, box and all, into your garden.

This approach is also perfect for kids. It'll teach them to care for a garden—keep those seedlings thinned out, don't forget to water, be patient—on a small scale before they move to a bigger space.

Add some sunshine to your life with a … *windowsill herb planter*

Isn't the idea of herbs growing along your kitchen windowsill divine? I love the idea of snipping off a few bits of fresh basil or cilantro to throw into whatever's cooking.

With cardboard, you can have your herbs inexpensively, too. Line up small boxes—shoe boxes are one option—in a window that gets good light and fill with soil and herbs. You'll be snipping and clipping in no time.

Stack 'em side by side to create a …*shoe box garden*

Finally, there's a good use for all those empty shoe boxes that've been filling up your closets for no reason! One of our photographers eagerly volunteered his wife's shoe box collection for our tests.

Keep in mind that most shoe boxes aren't very deep, so you'll need to choose items that don't need a lot of growing space. Lettuce, petite carrots and herbs are all good options.

For a cleaner appearance, we liked leaving the lids on our shoe boxes and cutting a rectangle into the top. Then just add your soil and plants. You can put a shoe box garden in practically any corner of your yard or patio. It's also a good project to do with kids, because it's easy to manage. They can really take ownership of their small plots.

Try a new way to start a...
square foot garden

Square foot gardening keeps growing in popularity, and with good reason: This technique lets you grow more in less space. I use it in my own backyard, and it works beautifully.

We're giving the method a new spin, though, encouraging you to use cardboard boxes to mark off your "squares" instead. Sure, most boxes aren't perfect squares, but they don't need to be. Add your boxes to a raised bed or an empty space in your yard. Follow the guidelines on how many plants to grow in each square foot; just reconfigure a bit if your boxes are bigger or smaller. Then you're off.

Have kids try this method, too. My son and daughter love having their own spaces and planning what to put in each square.

IS CARDBOARD OK?

The author of *The Truth About Gardening Remedies*, Jeff Gillman, has been debunking garden myths for years. We asked him about cardboard gardening.

ARE THERE ANY CONCERNS ABOUT USING CARDBOARD IN THE GARDEN?
The biggest problem with cardboard is that it will break down pretty rapidly. Directly in the compost pile, it will last only a couple of weeks. In the garden, it breaks down a little more slowly. So keep in mind that it probably won't last longer than a growing season.

DO YOU HAVE TO WORRY ABOUT FORMALDEHYDE IN THE GLUE USED ON CARDBOARD?
The formaldehyde is at such a low level that it really shouldn't do damage. Furthermore, as time goes on, the amount of formaldehyde will certainly decrease.

IS IT OK TO GROW VEGETABLES IN CARDBOARD?
Yes, though do be aware of what the cardboard held before you use it. If it was used for shipping industrial chemicals, for example, it might be best to avoid it. But in general, cardboard should be fine.

IS IT OK TO LEAVE CARDBOARD IN THE GARDEN TO BREAK DOWN ON ITS OWN?
Yes. Cardboard is really nothing more than ground-up and processed trees, so it returns to the soil the same as any wood mulch would.

FREE
garden makeovers

If you've ever hesitated before throwing something away—cracked dishes, broken toys, old sneakers—you'll love these cute and sometimes funky ideas. Gardeners tend to be natural recyclers. With these 10 household items, you can add whimsy to your backyard for free. That will leave room in your budget to splurge on more important things—like plants!

BY CRYSTAL RENNICKE

turn a wine bottle into a feeder!

Wine bottles

Description: A little wine can provide welcome therapy after an afternoon of battling weeds or pesky critters, and the bottle itself can dress up the garden, especially if it has a cool shape or color.

Ordinary uses: Add a hummingbird feeding tube and design your own feeder with some copper tubing and embellishments. (Check out the project at *birdsandblooms. com/hummingbirds* for ideas.) Or fill the bottle and insert it upside down into a pot to water plants while you're on vacation. The corks? Turn 'em into fun plant markers.

Extraordinary ideas: Flip bottles upside down and plant them around your garden as cutting-edge edging. Or insert a wick and some oil in each bottle and place them throughout your garden as lanterns for a garden party.

Suitcases

Description: If your old luggage has seen better days, it might be best suited to a destination close to home: your backyard.

Ordinary uses: Keep tools, pots and garden supplies organized in oversize suitcases.

Extraordinary idea: Open a suitcase, add soil, and plant your favorite herbs for a fanciful herb garden.

GLASS WITH CLASS.
Here's a fun, free, festive idea for keeping beds in line: Plant wine bottles upside down and use 'em for edging. You'll love the look!

Garden hose

Description: Some might put a leaky one out to pasture, but a holey hose makes a handy helper.

Ordinary uses: Make it a soaker hose for the garden, or use it to outline a new garden bed before digging.

Extraordinary idea: Coil it up, add some pretty ribbon or paint—and your friends will ask where you got that amazing outdoor wreath.

Tin cans

Description: One quick walk around the neighborhood on recycling-pickup day will get you lots. What they can do in the garden is almost limitless.

Ordinary uses: They make perfect collars to protect plants from cutworms. Flatten one or more beneath a ripening squash or watermelon to keep the fruit from rotting on the ground.

Extraordinary idea: Hosting a garden party? Fill a few cans with colorful flowers and hang them with string for informal bouquets that guests will find irresistible.

Tires

Description: Run over another nail? Don't discard those trashed tires— give them a new spin in the garden.

Ordinary uses: Paint tires in bold colors, then add plants or vegetables for distinctive containers. Or place the tires around young trees to protect the trees from the mower.

Extraordinary idea: Turn tires into unique garden chairs. Stack them up, fill with soil, and plant moss or grass inside for a neat seat that will delight your garden visitors.

2-liter plastic bottles

Description: Even if you don't drink soft drinks, your neighbors probably do. Ask around; chances are you'll find lots of them at your disposal.

Ordinary uses: Cut off the bottoms to make scoops for birdseed or grass seed, or use for starting seeds and protecting seedlings.

Extraordinary idea: Cut large holes in the bottles lengthwise, and you can grow just about anything inside. Try planting several with various herbs and hang them along a wall for a handy, inexpensive kitchen garden.

Plastic cups

Description: Singer Toby Keith made the song *Red Solo Cup* a country favorite, but this everyday item is more than a one-hit wonder.

Ordinary uses: Keep German yellow jackets at bay when you're dining outside by filling a cup with sugar

CREATIVE CANS. Leave tin cans plain or dress them up with paint, decorative paper or fabric. Then add a few flowers or herbs. It's an easy way to grow flowers, and it has a rustic charm.

help seedlings thrive!

HERBS WITH GARDEN FORK, GAP PHOTOS / LYNN KEDDIE; HANGING CAN PLANTER, GAP PHOTOS / JANET JOHNSON; FABRIC-COVERED CAN, GAP PHOTOS / FRIEDRICH STRAUSS; BOTTLE, RDA-MKF; ROW 5, GAP PHOTOS / GRAHAM STRONG;

water, covering it with foil, and poking a hole in the foil so they will find it. Plastic cups also make super seed starters.

Extraordinary idea: Cover cups with prettily patterned fabric. Using a string of white Christmas lights, put a bulb through an X cut in the bottom of each cup, then hang the whole thing in your yard. This is a bright idea for an after-dark party.

Table forks

Description: Ready to stick a fork in your old silverware? Put it back to work in the garden. Mismatched, funky-handled forks are a cinch to find at flea markets and secondhand stores.

Ordinary uses: Dig up pesky weeds with a table fork, or use it for small-scale gardening tasks, such as planting or digging in containers.
Extraordinary idea: Stick laminated seed packets between the tines for one-of-a-kind plant markers.

Kitchen bowls

Description: Most cooks have a few bowls that've seen better days. If you're due to treat yourself to some new mixing bowls, use your old ones in the garden!

Ordinary uses: Drill holes for drainage and pot up some plants. Or use an old basin to hold tools, seed packets and more while you work in the garden.
Extraordinary idea: Make mushrooms! Paint the bowls in solids, spots or stripes, turn them upside down and set each one on a wood scrap to resemble a growing field of colorful fungi.

Costume jewelry

Description: If you don't have your own collection, your mom or friends probably will. When a former favorite breaks, or just outwears its welcome as a bracelet, pin or necklace, think of it as the start of some garden art.
Ordinary uses: Gather some baubles and bangles and put them in planters as decorative mulch.
Extraordinary idea: Bedazzle everything! Use glue plus bits and pieces of old finery to decorate hummingbird feeders, pots (below), plant markers, rain barrels, compost bins, etc. Nothing is off-limits!

KITCHEN TO GARDEN. Old bowls, pans and more are all fair game to reuse outside as planters.

glass in the garden

Add some color to your backyard decor with these unique glass flowers. BY POLLY WILSON

Recycle mismatched plates, bowls or candleholders into a beautiful glass flower for your garden. It will definitely be a showstopper. The best part of this project is that you can use any style of glass plates or bowls you have on hand and paint them any colors you want. And this kind of flower requires no watering!

STEP 1. Clean all glass thoroughly with alcohol wipes and let it dry.
STEP 2. Use either a sponge or paintbrush to paint the glass pieces, covering completely. If you want, add details like stripes, circles or petals. A couple of layers might be necessary to get full coverage. Use the markers or pens to add small details.
STEP 3. Bake the glass pieces according to the directions on the paint bottles. (In general, bake at 325 degrees on the top rack for about 20 minutes.) But be careful: Very thin plates can break in the oven. And be sure to open your windows or turn on the exhaust fan, because the paints can have a strong odor when baking. Turn off the oven, and let the glass pieces cool completely before removing them.
STEP 4. Lay the largest plate flat on a covered surface. Apply silicone to the bottom of the next largest piece and press it down onto your base plate.
STEP 5. Continue applying silicone to the bottom of each of the smaller pieces until the flower is assembled. Let the whole piece dry overnight.

supplies

- 3 glass plates, bowls or dishes in different sizes
- 1 glass candleholder, salt or pepper shaker, or small vase (for center of the flower)
- 1 small vase with at least one flat side
- Alcohol wipes
- Glass paint
- Paintbrushes or sponges
- Markers or pens for glass
- Clear, waterproof silicone
- Metal or PVC pipe

STEP 6. The next day, apply silicone to a flat side of the small vase and, holding the vase upside down, press it to the back of the flower. This will serve as the mount that fits over the pipe for display purposes. Let the silicone dry overnight.
STEP 7. Pound the pipe into the ground, slip the flower over the pipe and stand back to admire your work. Now make a couple more—they look dazzling in groups of two or three!

GLAMOUR IN THE GARDEN. Add a bit of pizzazz to your flower bed art by incorporating faux rhinestones and glitter paint into your design.

weekend wreath

Make a beautiful living wreath in just three easy steps!

supplies

- **Ready-made sphagnum peat moss wreath (preferably with a hanger attached)**
- **Basin or washtub**
- **Topiary pins**
- **Shears**
- **Assorted herbs or flowers (we used chives, purple basil, sweet basil, Cuban oregano, feverfew and tricolor sage)**

STEP 1. Half-fill a large basin or tub with water and set it on a flat, sturdy surface. Dip the wreath inside and splash water on it. Let the wreath soak for a few seconds, until it's damp enough for planting.

To make your own wreath, buy sphagnum peat moss and pack it into a wire form. Then experiment with different shapes and sizes. Just make sure the hanging hardware supports the weight of the finished wreath.

STEP 2. Before you begin planting, arrange the plants according to color and size around the wreath to get a good idea of the finished product.

When you're satisfied, use your thumbs to make small holes where you can insert the plants. In the wreath above, chives were planted first because they occupy the outermost edge. Bushier herbs, like basil and oregano, were added next. Continue to add plants until your wreath is full.

STEP 3. Secure plants with topiary pins. The pins keep the plants in place and allow you to position foliage to help cover up bare spots. The plants grow while maintaining the shape of the wreath. Snip any unruly plants with shears, and hang your finished wreath on a wall or door. Planning to harvest fresh herbs from it regularly? Display it in the kitchen in a sunny spot.

jam jar garden lights

*Light up your backyard with this project
from a new family-friendly garden crafts book.*

With some beads, pens, sand and a tea light, you can turn a boring old jam jar into a pretty night-light for the garden. If you use a citronella candle, you will even find it helps ward off mosquitoes and other biting insects.

supplies

- Old jam jar
- Acrylic paint pens
- Thin garden wire, 20 in. (50 cm) long
- Glass, porcelain or plastic beads
- Play sand
- Plastic container or glass jar with lid
- Food coloring, optional
- Citronella tea light

STEP 1. Decorate your old jar using acrylic paint pens, and leave it to dry. Here, we have decorated the jar with lots of pretty flowers, but you can paint on any design that you like.

STEP 2. Make a loop at one end of the wire and thread on the beads from the other end until half the wire is covered (the loop will stop the beads from slipping off).

STEP 3. Wrap the unbeaded part of the wire around the neck of the jar, twisting the wire where it overlaps to secure it. Bend the beaded section to form a handle, leaving a little clear wire at the end. Hook this under the neck wire and then twist it to keep the handle securely in place.

STEP 4. If you want colored sand, pour a few handfuls of play sand into the bottom of another container or jar. Add a few drops of food coloring to the sand. Put the lid on tightly and shake it vigorously for 30 seconds.

STEP 5. Pour the sand into the bottom of the decorated jam jar. Then, gently drop the citronella tea light on top of the sand for lighting later on.

This kid-friendly project is from the book *Garden Crafts for Children* by Dawn Isaac (CICO Books, $19.95). Look for it at *cicobooks.com*.

Have a better backyard with these simple, money-saving ideas.

BY STACY TORNIO

What can you do in the garden for less than a dollar? That was the question that came up a few months ago as we were planning our summer issues.

At first it seemed impractical. After all, I can quickly drop more than $100 on one trip to the garden center. But then I started to brainstorm, and before I knew it I had a bunch of ideas. Many of them don't cost anything at all! Are you ready to save some money? After the amount I spent on plants this spring, I know I am!

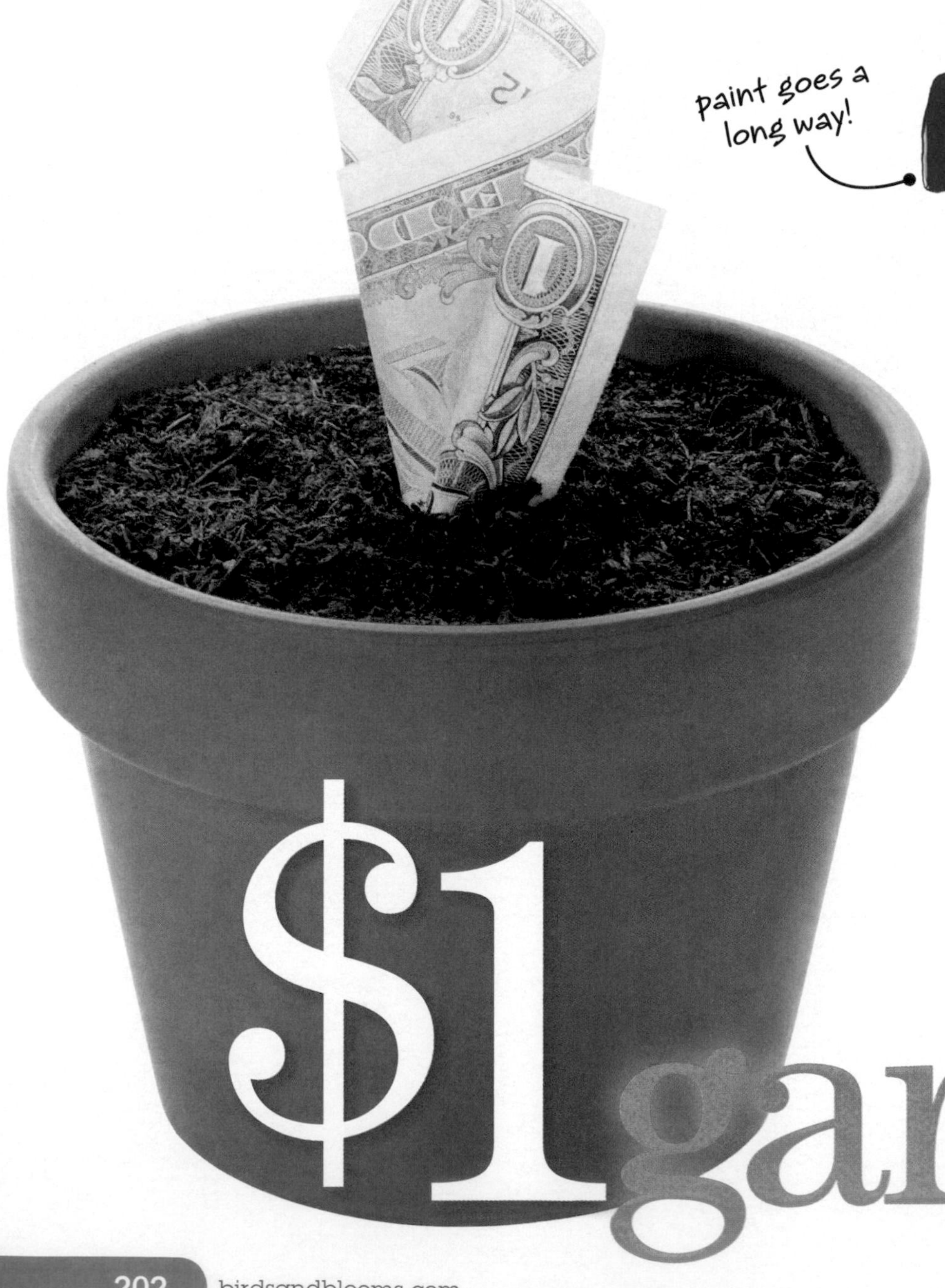

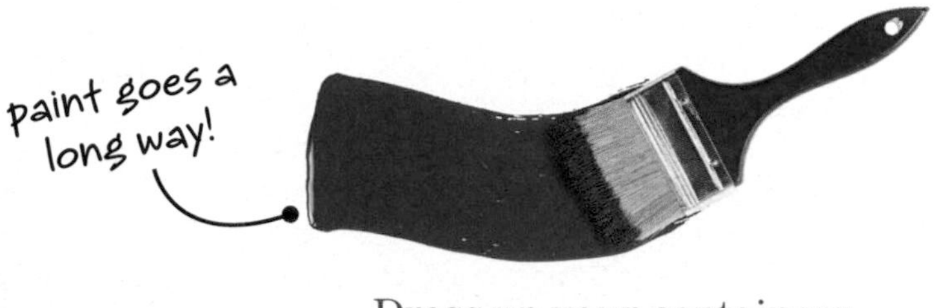

paint goes a long way!

Dress up your containers. I know you have some old, unused containers in your garage or shed. I'm the same way: I plant in my favorite containers first, so there are always a few that stay empty. Now is the time to bust them out and give them new life! Take a plain, ordinary container and dress it up. Use inexpensive items like paint to give it a new look. Or glue on pretty pebbles, twigs, letters—anything that strikes your fancy.

Plan your containers carefully. Yes, it's difficult not to get carried away with containers. You can easily spend a small fortune on preplanted containers or on plants to design them yourself. But here's where you can get ahead by doing a little planning. Choose your plants wisely! Challenge yourself to select a plant for

$1 garden

POT, STEVE CUKROV / SHUTTERSTOCK.COM; PAINTBRUSH, RT DESIGN STUDIO / SHUTTERSTOCK.COM; FLOWERS, PROVEN WINNERS / PROVENWINNERS.COM;

choose long bloomers

a dollar or less. (My choice would be petunias, like the red blooms above.) Then see how long it will last. If you pick long bloomers, you'll have color and beauty for five months or more!

Trade plants with a friend.

First get a group of your gardening friends together. Then have everyone throw in a buck, and buy some wine or a cheesecake to share. Set a date, and ask everyone to show up with a couple of plants they want to trade. You never know what you might end up with. Pass-along plants are some of the best, because they'll always remind you of your friend.

Add organic matter to your soil. This doesn't cost a

thing—you just need to remember to do it. You can use shredded paper or cardboard, leaves, or any kind of

mulch. If you're trying to improve the soil in a certain garden bed, this is an easy way to do it.

Grow shrubs from cuttings. Redtwig dogwood is one

of my favorite cutting success stories. Just snip off a branch, dip the end in rooting hormone, and place it in a good potting mix. Before you know it, that lone branch will send out roots, and you'll be well on your way to a whole new shrub. You can do this with other shrubs, too, but stick with old favorites, because new plants are patented and can't be propagated.

Overwinter your annuals.

Annuals are meant to grow for a single season, right? Maybe for some gardeners, but for those of you who are thrifty, here's another money-saving tip. You can either pot the entire plant and bring it inside over the winter, or take cuttings to get lots of new plants. Impatiens, for example, are easy to cut and root. For tropical varieties such as elephant ear and cannas, store while dormant and try starting them indoors in containers. Or grow them outdoors in containers on wheels. Then you can just roll them inside in fall.

solutions

Shop end-of-season sales.

Spring is hopping at the garden center, but the traffic slowly declines as the weather gets hotter. This is still a good time to buy plants. Look for perennials that drop to a dollar or less, add them to your garden immediately and keep them watered. These plants still have time to get established, and then they'll be ready to go next spring.

Learn the power of composting.

You can save oodles of money on potting soil by making your own rich compost. Starting and maintaining a compost pile is free. Just make sure to have a good mix of "green" plant-based food scraps and pest-free plants, along with "brown" material like cardboard, leaves and soil. Before you know it, it'll all break down to create nutrient-packed compost.

Plan a crop share.

Find out what a dollar's worth of seeds will get you. Then coordinate with friends and neighbors so that no two people plant the same thing. When it's time to harvest, split up the produce among the group members.

Sell your own plants online.

If you have a knack for starting seeds, buy a pack for a dollar and grow some plants. Then sell your plants online; try *craigslist.org*. You can also divide some of the plants in your garden to sell this way. Remember that you can't sell plants that are protected by patents, so you might want to check into this before selling new or trademarked varieties.

Buy plants with friends.

Everyone chips in a buck, then the group hits the garden center to buy in bulk. A dollar will go a lot further than you might think.

buy seeds and plants on clearance!

Use cardboard to start a new garden bed.

You can easily start a whole new garden bed using the power of cardboard. Just section off a spot in your lawn and layer cardboard, soil, shredded paper and mulch. You can do this now and then let it sit all fall and winter. Come spring, you'll have a brand-new garden bed ready for your plants. You'll find more cardboard-gardening ideas starting on page 186.

Get resources from the library.

Instead of spending a lot of money on new gardening books, go to your library instead. It is likely to have books aimed at your region, and browsing won't cost you a cent.

Save your own seeds.

Late in the summer, your favorite blooms start to go to seed. You can collect them straight from the plant if you'd like; an empty Tic Tac container is the perfect place to store them. Another way to collect seeds: Snip off a seed head and tie a paper bag around the top. Then hang it upside down for a few weeks. The seeds will dry and drop off on their own. Plant in fall or spring.

Take advantage of your local extension.

If you have a tough gardening question, look to your local Cooperative Extension. It often has hotlines or events featuring master gardeners who can offer answers. This is a free service, so use it!

Use a rain barrel.

Cut your watering bill by putting out your own rain barrel. Many communities offer rain barrels at a very low price, or no cost at all! Also, look online for someone who's getting rid of one. Just think of all the money you'll save on watering!

fresh ideas for CONTAINERS

Update your outdoor spaces with the latest ideas in container gardening.

BY CRYSTAL RENNICKE

Looking to expand your container garden repertoire? Give your ho-hum pots the boot and spice up your landscape with some of these new ideas. In no time at all, your yard can boast beautiful, stylish containers. Ready to dig in? Take a look at how to make these work for you.

Pick Your Perfect Pot

When you shop for containers, pick ones that reflect your personal style. Do you prefer a trusty terra-cotta pot, a contemporary low-bowl planter or a sturdy metal container?

Unconventional items—an oversize coffee mug, a watering can, a birdbath—add personality and flair. Scour your basement or garage for homemade containers, but make sure they have proper drainage. Drill a hole or two in the bottom if necessary.

If you can't find exactly what you want, personalize a pot with paint, mosaic tiles, beads or even some silly feet.

MIX IT UP. Try adding basil, cilantro or other herbs in your containers.

Have Fun With Plants

The rule of thumb when picking plants for easy-care containers is that they have similar light and moisture requirements. Aside from that, have fun! You could follow the "thriller-spiller-filler rule," making sure your pot contains a tall, eye-catching plant, a plant to fill in the container

DRESS IT UP. A little flair goes a long way with containers. Above, this colorful mosaic pot on a backyard table dresses up the entire area. Right, enliven a lackluster garden bed by nestling in a few bold pots.

and one to spill over the side. But really, anything goes. A few ideas:

Go bold. Command attention with a "wow" plant like an elephant ear, a small arborvitae or anything that offers interesting foliage or a ton of bright color. Make that plant the focus, and fill out the rest of the container with plants that complement it.

One pot, one color. Pick a favorite hue or color combination as your theme. For example, fill a metallic silver pot with purple flowers and a black sweet potato vine for a sophisticated look.

Color-coordinate. Remember learning about the color wheel back in art class? Make complementary colors work for you. Yellow and purple flowers create wonderful contrast when planted in earth-toned pottery. Orange blossoms pop in a cobalt-blue container.

Try minimalism. If you have a unique container, keep it simple and limit your mix to one or two plants. Even an ordinary planter can become a focal point when you go for a single species.

Think beyond the ordinary. Container gardening lets you experiment with plants you might not normally use. Try a container filled with succulents, or a combination of vegetables or edible ornamentals combined with annuals. Grow tropical plants like cannas, or ornamental grasses with coleus for a fabulous foliage display.

Share the Beauty

Butterflies and hummingbirds love nectar-producing flowers including verbena, aster, geraniums (below left) and salvia. Fill planters with these favorites and place them at different heights throughout the yard to encourage a variety of fliers to visit.

To create a multilayered look, set your containers on a tabletop, shelf or other raised surface so they're at eye level. When a winged creature flies in to investigate, you'll be certain to notice. Increase containers' impact by grouping them throughout the backyard. If you have a patio, position large containers to create a secluded, intimate area.

Plan for the Seasons

To ensure that your container lasts throughout the growing season, include plants with different bloom times. Those with interesting foliage fit the bill as well. And don't limit yourself to annuals. Perennials are ideal for pots, and shrubs are becoming more adaptable to containers. The Lo & Behold Blue Chip butterfly bush and the Midnight Wine weigela are a couple of compact shrubs that butterflies and hummingbirds happen to love.

Banish Watering Woes

Wouldn't it be nice not to have to worry about your containers while you're out of town, or even if you're just busy? Get water-wise with stylish self-watering containers and devices. One reliable trick that works for houseplants and containers alike is using a self-watering globe or a "plant nanny." A wine bottle or other water-filled vessel is placed upside down in the pot, allowing the water to flow into the soil as it dries.

You might also try a self-watering container. Newer varieties are pretty and practical, and they take the guesswork out of watering. All you have to do is fill the reservoir when it's empty.

GO VERTICAL. Never underestimate the importance of vertical accents. It's an eye-popping way to expand the visual benefits of your containers. Here, the dramatic height of this aloe elongates the blue container in the center, adding interest all around. In the inset, New Zealand flax looks striking by itself in a deck container.

Dig It!

Everyone is growing veggies this year. If you're intimidated by the thought of an abundant, sprawling garden, start small with your favorite vegetables in containers. Smaller varieties of veggies, including the new Spacemaster cucumber and Cherries Jubilee tomato, thrive in containers and are packed with flavor.

There are also herbs and ornamentals on the market that are suitable for small spaces and containers. Try the deep-purple Ruffles basil or a fiery ornamental pepper that will look festive long into fall. Grow them alone or combine them with flowers.

invite butterflies & hummingbirds

Include a compact butterfly bush in a container for a combination that nectar seekers will love.

A English Butterfly™ Peacock™ butterfly bush (1)
B Merlin's Magic coleus (1)
C Diamond Frost® euphorbia (1)
D Kalipso spurge (1)
E Sentimental Journey® betony (1)

stunning in the shade

Place this container in the shade. Include an elephant ear for height and a tropical feel, and fill in the container with red and pink plants for a pop of color.

A Upright elephant ear (1)
B Infinity® Pink New Guinea impatiens (1)
C Capricorn Rex begonia (1)
D Flamenco Tango cuphea (1)

CHAPTER 8

Perfect
photography

Take first-class photographs.
Discover ways that nature lovers can
use their cameras to raise wildlife
awareness. Master expert techniques
for capturing moving targets.

BLEEDING HEARTS, CAROL FREEMAN

dancing with
CRANES

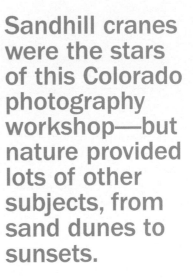

Sandhill cranes were the stars of this Colorado photography workshop—but nature provided lots of other subjects, from sand dunes to sunsets.

BY KIRSTEN SWEET

It was 5:30 on a chilly March morning, and we were on a mission. Eager photographers and birders were bundled up and crammed into four vehicles, along with cameras, lenses and tripods. We were racing against the sunrise to photograph greater sandhill cranes at Monte Vista National Wildlife Refuge in Colorado's San Luis Valley.

About 20 of us from all over the country were staying at the Zapata Ranch for a sandhill crane photography workshop. Thousands of the birds migrate through the wildlife refuge on their way from their winter home in New Mexico to breeding grounds in the northern U.S. and southern Canada.

Michael Forsberg and Dave Showalter, professional nature photographers and two of the nicest guys around, were our teachers and tour guides for the week, helping us hone our photography skills so that we could go home with the kind of photos we'd seen only in magazines.

In the Field

It was still dark when we reached our destination. As soon as our feet hit the pavement, we could hear their calls: The sandhill cranes were nearby. Hundreds of them had gathered at a small pond only a short distance in front of us. As the sun rose behind us, the view was remarkable.

The sunlit mountains cast their reflections on the water where the cranes rested, providing us with a perfect photo op.

Later in the day, we found the cranes feeding in a field. Here, we not only photographed the birds but observed and learned about their behavior. Sandhill cranes have strong family ties, and couples mate for life. Once Michael pointed out a few family groups, it was easy to see other groups of three or four—a mother, father and offspring.

But the best part of watching the cranes was getting to see their famous mating dance. Breeding pairs put on an amazing show of jumping, flapping and loud calls that make you think they're about to engage in a brutal fight, but it's actually their flamboyant way of courting.

Another Day, Another Photo

We spent our second day at Great Sand Dunes National Park (pictured at right), where the play between shadows and light is a photographer's dream. Here we roamed and explored the area on our own a bit. As a beginner, I took the opportunity to learn everything I could from Dave, who spotted a neat pair of trees as we drove in. He brought out his own

FAST FRIENDS. From left, Chris, Kirsten and Gini. Amazing sights, delicious dinners and exciting photos quickly bring people together.

top 5 nature photography spots to visit

Michael Forsberg helped compile this list of must-see Western hot spots.

1. PLATTE RIVER VALLEY, NEBRASKA. Visit this sandhill crane migration stopover in the spring and you'll see thousands of cranes fueling up in the meadows and farmlands near the river.

2. YELLOWSTONE AND GRAND TETON NATIONAL PARKS, WYOMING. It doesn't matter what time of year you visit—you won't be disappointed by the vast variety of wildlife, especially birds. The calliope hummingbird, western tanager and several raptors and wetland birds call this area home, as do hundreds of other species.

3. BADLANDS NATIONAL PARK AND BLACK HILLS, SOUTH DAKOTA. This is a meeting ground for several eastern and western species throughout the year. If you visit, keep your eyes peeled for mountain bluebirds, nuthatches and black-billed magpies.

4. ROCKY MOUNTAIN NATIONAL PARK, COLORADO. More than 250 kinds of birds have been reported in the park, which is known for its unique mountain species. Look for Wilson's, MacGillivray's and Virginia's warblers.

5. BOSQUE DEL APACHE NATIONAL WILDLIFE REFUGE, NEW MEXICO. Set on more than 50,000 acres along the Rio Grande, the refuge includes a 15-mile auto tour route where visitors can stop to view and photograph wildlife along the way.

CRANES IN FLIGHT. Capturing the image of birds in flight takes patience and practice. It's worth it, though, when you get a photo like the one above.

nature photo tips
Be a better photographer with these tricks.

TELL A STORY. Think of your photo as a story with a beginning, middle and end. Make sure the image has a foreground, middle ground and background.

LOOK FOR LINES. Lead-in lines make for memorable photos. Search for small roads, footprints, animal tracks in the mud or any other natural lines.

LIGHT MATTERS. It's worth the extra effort to catch the "golden hour" at dawn or dusk, when light has color and warmth. You'll be amazed at how shadows contribute to the beauty of a photo.

FOCUS ON INDIVIDUALS. Don't get distracted by a lot of activity. When photographing groups of birds, keep your camera focused on one bird for a while. Eventually, it will do something interesting.

MOVE AROUND. Walk around your subjects to get a different perspective. You might see a tree that makes a fantastic photo, but another angle may provide an even more spectacular view.

equipment and showed a small group of us how to set up an ideal shot focusing on some gold plants in the foreground, a couple of trees in the midground and the mountains and sky in the background.

Our evening photo session at the dunes was equally as breathtaking. We took a short hike down to Medano Creek, a seasonal stream that runs through the park. It was one of the most peaceful places I have ever been. We were lucky enough to spot horse tracks directly across from the creek, allowing our cameras to capture the lines of the tracks as they stretched over the dunes.

We stayed out that day, cameras in hand, until the sun set on the last dune and all the fresh air made us hungry enough to head back to the ranch for dinner.

Memories Last a Lifetime

For me, this workshop was as much about the memories I made with a group of strangers as it was about the scenery, birds and photos. Together, we laughed, shivered in the cold and witnessed some of nature's wonders. Would I go on a trip like this again? In a heartbeat.

try, try again

A wily bird gives this photographer an education in patience and flexibility.

STORY AND PHOTOS BY JIM MURTAGH

Pileated woodpeckers

One of my greatest lessons as a photographer started with a single bird perched on a cedar post. It was a male northern flicker, to be exact. His golden underside, elegant black spots and vibrant red patch seemed to beckon me to take a photo.

I grabbed my camera to snap a quick shot, but getting a good one became a tougher challenge than I expected. After a solid week, I finally got my photo, but not without a few setbacks—and some real-world education—along the way.

Starting With a Blind

Concealed within my portable camouflaged shooting blind, I thought it would be fairly simple to capture the perfect photo of the flicker perched up on the post. But it wasn't that easy. The relaxed bird I observed through binoculars did not want me to get closer, even in my blind. Every time I did, he flew from his perch.

Frustrated with my growing collection of blurry images, I knew I needed to change my technique. Instead of getting into the blind whenever I had spare time, I made up my mind to enter before sunrise and wait for the bird to arrive.

This simple change appeased the flicker, and now I could watch him search for morsels to eat as he explored every crevice in the post, pecking with his long bill and probing with his eel-like tongue.

My confidence building, I set out to take my ideal image. The flicker paused midway up the column. It wasn't the composition at the top of the post that I had imagined, but I felt compelled to try for any photo at this

Northern flicker

Tufted titmouse

House wren

Red-bellied woodpecker

take it to the next level
Jim shares his top three tips.

EXPAND. There's no rule that says backyard birding must take place in your own backyard. Ask your neighbors and friends if you can sit in their yards to take pictures for a few hours. People are flattered when someone appreciates the birding landscapes they worked hard to design, and different habitats attract different bird species.

EMBRACE. You can reap the rewards of any weather. Rain, snow and fog add drama and saturate the colors in your photos. Birds tend to feed heavily just before and soon after a storm, providing you with abundant opportunities.

ENGAGE. Shoot video in addition to still photos. Most cameras capture spectacular video, and many digital picture frames play movie files. Don't hesitate to switch from still to video mode on your camera when you catch a robin eating a worm or see a bluebird (such as the one below) taking a bath.

point. I slowly began to reposition my lens, and then—gone.

The camera movement startled the bird, and once more I had nothing to show for my efforts. My patience had been tested and I'd failed, so I aimed for the top of the cedar log again. And this time I promised myself that I would wait for the shot to come to me instead of forcing it.

Lesson Learned
A skilled teacher, the flicker returned to see if I understood the lesson. He bounced all around the post, pausing here and there, teasing me to see if I would move. I didn't.

Finally, the bird took his spot at the top of the post, just the way I first saw him. As I pressed the shutter release halfway, the

autofocus engaged, the gears in the lens adjusted and then the flicker darted away.

Thus began the final lesson: No noise allowed, not even the seemingly innocuous purr of the lens focusing. I knew I was dependent on my camera's autofocus system but had never found it a liability. Until this flicker arrived, manual focus had seemed antiquated, so I never acquired the skill. Learning to focus manually took some practice—well, a lot of practice—but it has made me a more proficient photographer.

After six days of ups and downs, I eventually snapped the photo. My skittish subject demanded that I adapt to the situation and acquire new skills if I wanted to succeed. So I did.

every day in **may**

THE SIGHTS OF MAY.
When photographer and writer Carol Freeman sets out on her monthlong photography quest in spring, bleeding hearts are just one of the blooms she expects to see.

Join this photographer in a monthlong search for warblers and wilderness. BY CAROL FREEMAN

May is one of the most glorious months for nature photography. At least it is where I live, near Chicago.

More than eight years ago, I was surprised and thrilled to realize that I had no obligations in May, so I decided to dedicate the entire month to nature photography. I set out with my camera every single day, rain or shine.

I enjoyed the experience so much that I've continued the tradition every year since. It's become my retreat—my time to reconnect with nature and to witness the miracle of spring. I tell everyone, "I'm busy. Call me in June." This is May. It's my time to feel alive again.

May 17
Magnolia warbler

The whole thing started because of warblers...

They hold a special place in my heart because they're so elusive and so beautiful this time of year.

So when I started that first year of photography in May, my main goal was to find warblers. I'd never had much luck seeing or photographing these tiny wonders from the neotropics. After all, they pass through Chicago so very quickly—here one day and gone the next—on the way to their breeding grounds up north.

I started learning more about them: what their migration patterns are, which ones prefer treetops, which ones will fly lower. Doing my homework paid off, because I did find a few warblers that first year. But I learned and saw so much more along the way.

These days, I'm still learning and seeing new things. I'll admit it can be hard to get outside every single day in May, especially early in the month. It's easy to think up an excuse: It's cold, it's windy, it's cloudy, I'm tired, I don't have time. But then I always tell myself: *Just 15 minutes. I can find 15 minutes to take some photos.*

To make it easier, I often shoot in my own yard. I grow native plants and get a surprising amount of wildlife on my suburban patio. Even when it's cold, windy or rainy, I'm rewarded with natural wonders I could never have imagined: bejeweled, dewy spiderwebs; treetop-dwelling birds visiting me at eye level; flowers bowing under the drops of new rain.

By the time I hit mid-May, I really start looking forward to the adventure each day brings. Then the month flies, and suddenly it's over before I know it.

Along the way, I keep a journal to note the temperature, wind, cloud cover and every bird and flower I spot. Each year I notice new species and visit new locations, but I'm always amazed to see the beauty and diversity close to home.

May 4
Common yellowthroat

Trout lily

Shooting star

Trillium

Spring beauty

May 11
Blackburnian warbler

go on your own adventure

Whether you try photographing for an entire week, month or year, Carol shares her secrets for making the most of your time outside.

1. I FIND THAT WARBLERS LIKE WATER, so I'll often sit by a stream or river and wait for the birds to work their way through. (They do seem to come in waves.)

2. PLAN AHEAD BY CHECKING out nearby locations you'd like to visit. This will save you time.

3. PROCESS YOUR IMAGES EACH DAY, and update your log or journal if you keep one. It's much easier and faster to do this regularly.

4. PLAN WHAT YOU'LL DO ON THOSE WINDY, rainy or cold days. Can you visit a nearby arboretum or indoor nursery?

5. DON'T UNDERESTIMATE THE FASCINATING THINGS you can find in your own backyard. Raindrops and dewdrops make for magical photos!

6. SET UP A BIRD FEEDER, a birdbath and a few native plants, and you'll have countless things to photograph every day.

7. BE STILL. Wildlife often disperse at your approach, so find a seat in a likely area and wait for the birds to come to you.

8. READ UP ON THE BIRDS you'd like to see, and learn their patterns so you know where to photograph them.

getting a late start

Better late than never rings true for this son of a wildlife photographer.

STORY AND PHOTOS BY RUSSELL CRONBERG

Photography should have been a shoo-in for me as a career or hobby. While I was growing up, my parents owned both a camera store and a one-hour film-processing lab. I had every opportunity to get serious about taking pictures, yet for some reason I was never interested.

Despite my utter indifference to stepping behind the camera, though, I was always a huge fan of photography.

I loved looking at the images captured by my dad, an accomplished wildlife photographer. But his work seemed impossible to replicate.

Whenever I got the slightest inclination to try taking my own pictures, I was always quick to dismiss the idea. I made up excuses: It's too difficult. I don't have the patience. I can't get my images as sharp or as colorful.

Then, one day, it happened. My parents had sold the family business 18 years earlier, but my interest in photography suddenly developed with one little trip.

My dad is the one to blame. He wanted to check out a wetland area he had read about. Since it was near where I lived, he invited me to come along, then offered me the use of his spare camera and zoom lens.

Brown pelican

Anna's hummingbird

Great egret

Black-necked stilt

lessons learned

Russell shares some of the tips he has picked up over the years.

GO OFF THE BEATEN PATH. Many times I'll be shooting with a group of photographers all in one area, but then I'll venture off on my own. This often helps me get more interesting shots than the rest of the group.

TAKE LOTS OF PHOTOS. Most people don't take as many as they should. It's a numbers game. The more shots you get, the greater your chance of capturing that special image.

WALK AROUND. Sure, a tripod can be a big help, but don't be afraid to photograph on the go. Wildlife photography doesn't always have to be in one place.

INVEST IN BACKYARD FEEDING STATIONS. This will help attract songbirds and hummingbirds. Even though they're not big game, they make wonderful practice subjects.

At first there was nothing much to photograph, and I began to regret having to carry a heavy, bulky camera for no good reason. But it wasn't long before something caught my eye.

About 20 feet away, near the water's edge, a graceful great blue heron stood absolutely motionless. With my adrenaline level quickly rising, I carefully lifted up the camera, composed the shot and—*click!*—I had just snapped my first wildlife photograph, and was immediately hooked.

This happened only a few years ago, so I've had a relatively short time behind the camera. But in that time, I've been privileged to photograph some pretty amazing creatures in beautiful places and to meet some wonderful people.

Now I look forward to my future as a wildlife photographer. No matter how advanced I might become, I realize there is always something more to learn. I might have started this hobby a bit later than some, but I relish every moment.

winter wonders

This husband-and-wife photo team shares insider tips for winter nature photos.

STORY AND PHOTOS BY SUSAN AND RICHARD DAY

Just because the weather is cold and dreary doesn't mean you can't be outside with your camera. Some of the most beautiful bird photos are taken in winter—just look at this story and past winter issues of *Birds & Blooms*!

Shooting in winter does take a little more planning than fair-weather photography, but here are a couple of pointers to get you started.

Be Prepared

Have everything ready before it snows. Scout out potential sites to return to during or after a snowfall: an old barn, mill, covered bridge, country road, mountainside, stream or park.

Then find an area with evergreen trees or bushes with berries, such as winterberry or holly, which always look pretty when covered in snow. If you're after birds, place a feeder or two nearby so they can get used to feeding there. (The greenery also protects them from predators while they eat.)

You can take pictures of birds on the feeders with a nice evergreen background, or when they perch on the boughs or bushes.

Think Holiday

Even if it's not Christmas, set out a couple of holiday props, like a wreath, garland or some colorful bows, on evergreens, fences or barns or near bird feeders. You can use these photos for next year's cards, or frame them to decorate your home in winter.

Look at last year's holiday cards for ideas.

Know the Weather

When snow is in the forecast, get your camera gear ready the night before so you can be outside the next day photographing the fresh, clean snowfall. Keep in mind that the whiteness can fool your in-camera light meter, making your snow pictures look blue or gray. You can compensate for this by opening up 1-2 stops on a manual camera, or using your exposure compensation on an automatic camera.

Though some winter scenic photos look gorgeous with white snow and blue skies, sometimes the sunshine produces harsh shadows. Watch for these when taking the photo. If they're distracting, change your composition and try using the shadows as patterns against the snow.

On cloudy days, avoid taking photos that show sky, because it will look gray or white. Instead, focus on small things like pinecones, bird close-ups or part of an old building with snowy details.

THE WHOLE PACKAGE. Set up a suet feeder in a wreath or use berries to attract picture-perfect birds, such as this downy woodpecker and American goldfinch.

THE POWER OF RED. A little bit of red goes a long way, as seen with these berries and a female northern cardinal or the big bow and a blue jay (below). Bottom right, this photographer works to get the perfect snowy scene.

Get Outside

An impromptu walk in a park or even in your own backyard can reveal surprises like frosty ferns or animal tracks in fresh snow. Also, try photographing during a snowfall. Even though the snowflakes can be distracting, you may get some moody, wintry photos. Keep the shutter speed fast (1/250 or higher) so the snowflakes don't streak.

Watch the Birds

You'll see different birds at feeders in winter than in summer. After it snows, birds congregate at feeders for fast food. Attach an evergreen or berry branch above a feeder: Birds tend to perch a bit higher before eating, so this is a good way

to capture them on a snowy or icy perch. Sprinkle a little seed or suet on evergreens so the birds will perch there. You'll get better photos if the birds don't see you, so use a blind, or photograph from inside your house or another building.

Stay Warm

Obviously, you need to use your fingers to operate your equipment, so a thin pair of glove liners under fingerless gloves or mittens will help you focus and use the dials and buttons on your camera.

Wear layers of clothing and cozy socks and boots so you'll be comfortable outside. And make sure to have extra batteries handy in a pocket so they'll stay warm, too.

perfect photography   **227**

Mountain bluebirds
Photo by George Sanker /
NPL / Minden Pictures

Blue jay
Photo by Richard Day /
Daybreak Imagery

Northern saw-whet owl
Photo by Mathew Levine /
Flickr / Getty Images

Common yellowthroat
Photo by Patty Jennings

Green tree frog in a daylily
Photo by John Switzer

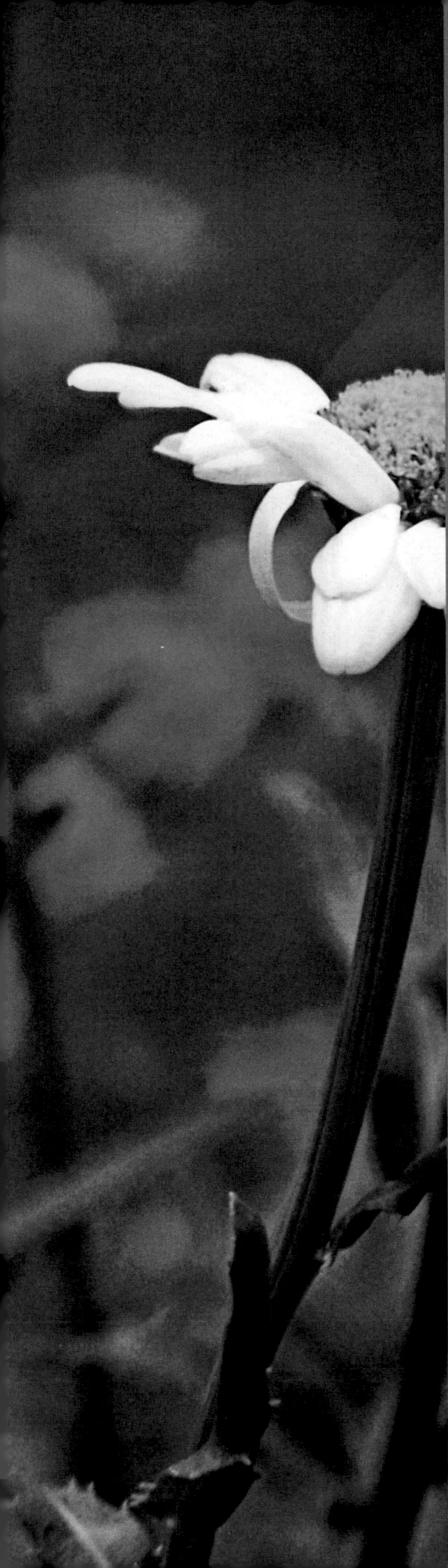

CHAPTER 9

Butterflies
& beyond

Catch a glimpse of butterflies' lives throughout the year. Brush up on ways to identify beneficial insects. Feed winged wonders in your own garden with native plants and treats from the kitchen.

PAINTED LADY. DENNIS STROMBERG

butterfly

"Plant it and they will come."

Believe it or not, it really is that simple when you're talking about butterfly host plants. Scatter dill seeds among your lovely cosmos, and soon you'll see swallowtails. Plant a patch of milkweed, and you're bound to get monarchs. Have an out-of-the-way corner for nettles? Get ready to welcome red admirals. Butterfly gardening truly is this easy, yet it's often confusing. Myths about it abound, so let's set the story straight.

gardening MYTHS

Discover the truth about attracting these beauties, and increase your chance of success.

BY SALLY ROTH

LOOK FOR HOSTS. Host plants are essential for any butterfly garden. Black swallowtails need dill for their caterpillars (inset).

MYTH The best way to get more butterflies in my yard is to plant plenty of nectar flowers.

TRUTH It's true that to nectar-seeking butterflies, the more flowers, the better. But it's even more important for us wildlife gardeners to think ahead. Yes, they'll show up at any yard for nectar, but those butterflies dancing over the daisies need a place to lay their eggs. Supply host plants tailored to the tastes of the caterpillars, and you will enjoy more butterflies for years to come.

MYTH Habitats such as forests, meadows and marshes aren't necessary to butterflies, since they spend all their time flitting about looking for flowers.

TRUTH Sure, butterflies may range miles afield to visit flowers. But when it's time to start the next generation, many species are highly dependent on a particular kind of habitat. This is often where the plants that their caterpillars eat are found.

For butterflies, it's host plants that determine the place they call home. Some, such as viceroys (hosts: willows and poplars) and painted ladies (hosts: thistles, mallows and various legumes), range widely.

a welcoming way station

To help supplement wild plants, Monarch Watch has developed a way station program for schools, businesses, gardeners and anyone else with a bit of space to grow host and nectar plants. A kit containing seeds and suggestions costs $16. Visit *monarchwatch.org/waystations* to learn more.

Other butterflies, including many species that are in decline, rely on host plants that grow only in certain areas. The gorgeous black-and-white zebra swallowtail, for instance, needs young pawpaw trees to support its brood, so it's found near the moist, low woods where the trees grow. The Baltimore checkerspot is a wetland species, because that's where one of its favorite host plants, turtlehead (*Chelone glabra*), naturally grows.

MYTH Butterfly populations are doing fine. Any yearly differences are only normal cycles.
TRUTH Sadly, many butterflies in North America are in decline, just as they are in Great Britain and elsewhere in the world.

Butterflies that rely on habitat-specific host plants are among the most threatened. If a bulldozer scrapes off their favorite patch of host plants, they may be out of luck.

The Karner blue, a dainty little beauty, relies on a lupine (*Lupinus perennis*) that grows in the sandy prairies, lakeshores and pine barrens of the Northeast and Midwest. And these lupines are disappearing fast. Fritillary species that depend on native violets are declining, too. For monarchs, it's the loss of milkweed in herbicide-sprayed farm fields that's suspected to be an important cause of their falling numbers.

MYTH Adding host plants to a backyard is such a small effort that it won't be a significant help to local butterfly populations.
TRUTH One small step for butterflies in the backyard is one giant leap for butterflies everywhere! Our plantings may be small, but with so many of us helping butterflies, those efforts add up in a big way.

MYTH Host plants aren't as pretty as the flowers planted for nectar. They look weedy.
TRUTH Host plants can be just as showy as garden flowers. Bright-orange butterfly weed, pink swamp milkweed, pink or white turtlehead, western bleeding heart, blue bird's-foot violet, hollyhocks, snapdragons, nasturtiums: All are gorgeous garden flowers as both host plants and nectar

sources. Bronze fennel and dill offer pretty foliage.

MYTH Caterpillars will chew host plants to bits, and who wants that in their garden?

TRUTH Once you spot your first butterflies-to-be, you won't mind the nibbled look at all. It's a sure sign of success! You'll find yourself checking the progress of the brood day by day, looking forward to more beautiful wings.

MYTH Butterflies are highly specific about which plant they'll lay their eggs on. Many use just one particular kind of plant.

TRUTH This is true for some species but way off the mark for many others. Think plant family, rather than species. For instance, mustard family plants—from broccoli to arugula to nasturtiums—are perfect for cabbage whites. The entire milkweed family will attract monarchs. Willows bring in mourning cloaks, and elms attract eastern commas.

MYTH Only native plants are used as host plants.

TRUTH Native plants are always a fine choice for butterflies, but non-natives that belong to the same family are often adopted by some species, too.

Dill, parsley and fennel got their start around the Mediterranean. Yet the larvae of the black and anise swallowtail will happily munch them all.

English plantain, a common imported weed, hosts buckeye butterflies and other species along its wide track. Monarchs will accept any milkweed species, no matter how far from its native origin it's growing.

MYTH If I want to attract fritillaries, all I have to do is plant violets or pansies for host plants.

TRUTH Here's where natives are vital. These butterflies are picky about where they put their eggs, and

prickly subject

Nettles are the preferred host plant of the widespread red admiral butterfly, but not everyone welcomes a patch of stinging nettles in the yard. Luckily, these pretty fliers are just as fond of false nettle (*Boehmeria cylindrica*, right), a nonirritating plant. Both types of nettles spread fast, so plant them in an area where you won't fret if they grow out of bounds.

finding fritillary food

Want to find native violets to host fritillaries in your garden, but don't know what's native to your area? Here are three easy ways to track them down.

1. Visit the nearest native plant nursery.

2. Watch for plant sales held by native plant enthusiasts or botanic gardens.

3. Power up your Web browser and search for your county and state and the words "native violets." More than one native in your region? Try any or all!

native violets are the plants their larvae chomp. A few species have also adopted non-native Johnny jump-ups (*Viola tricolor*), but it's the native violets they most prefer.

And this is where we gardeners can make a notable difference. The gorgeous regal fritillary and some of its other fritillary relatives are declining, because those native violets have been turned to the plow or destroyed by development. By nurturing native violets, such as bird's-foot violet (*Viola pedata*) for the regal fritillary, we can provide an oasis in our gardens for the upcoming young.

Be sure to choose violets that are native to your region, not just "American natives." With dozens of fritillary species ranging here and there in North America, regional tastes matter. In the Midwest, for instance, bird's-foot violet is a good choice—but not so in the West, where the fritillaries prefer yellow-flowered Nuttall's violet (*Viola nuttalli*).

MYTH Planting a host for a butterfly that doesn't live in my area will attract them to my yard; they'll seek the plant at egg-laying time.
TRUTH Not likely, if the butterfly's natural range is far away. But it

could make a difference if every neighbor along the way pitched in as well. Some experts believe the pipevine swallowtail expanded its range in response to the popularity of Dutchman's pipe (*Aristolochia* spp.) as a porch vine.

MYTH There are too many host plants to know; no one size fits all.
TRUTH Can you remember three? Milkweeds, dill and hollyhocks: They're a great place to start, and all have wide appeal. Then fill in the gaps with native plants. Chances are some butterfly (or moth) will be happy to call them home.

salvia for butterflies

BY JILL STAAKE

These varieties will bring them fluttering to your backyard.

As I flip through seed catalogs and plan my gardens for the year, I'm on the lookout for new types of salvia I can add to my butterfly garden. Most salvia, commonly known as sage, produces wonderful nectar flowers for butterflies (many draw hummingbirds, too), and it's easy to start from seed.

Here are a few varieties to look for. The list is by no means comprehensive, but it does include some of the more widely available species and cultivars.

SALVIA COCCINEA (aka tropical sage or scarlet sage). One of the easiest salvias to grow from seed, it's an annual that may reseed. Plant it in full to partial sun. Look for cultivars Summer Jewel Red and Coral Nymph.

SALVIA ELEGANS (aka pineapple sage). This salvia grows best from cuttings rather than seed. Get plants from your local nursery. It is usually grown as an annual, but is hardy in Zones 8 to 11. Plants produce showy red flowers with pineapple-scented foliage.

SALVIA GREGGII (aka autumn sage). A Southwestern native, this salvia is unbeatable for drought and heat tolerance. Plant in Zones 6 to 11 in full sun. Wild Thing is a cultivar worth trying.

SALVIA FARINACEA (aka mealycup sage). Native to Mexico and Texas, this variety does best in full sun to partial shade in very hot climates. It is somewhat drought-tolerant and is grown as an annual in cold regions and as a perennial in Zones 8 to 10. It's available in blue, white or a blue-white mix.

WHAT ABOUT THE SALVIA AT GARDEN STORES?
Salvia splendens is one of the more common species you'll find in nurseries and seed catalogs. It comes in an incredibly wide variety of colors, and it's frequently sold as a butterfly magnet. While this may be true in some cases, most varieties have been so extensively hybridized for color and growth habit that their nectar value is greatly diminished. The bottom line? It's a lovely ornamental plant, and if you find a variety that lures butterflies, that's the icing on the cake. But if you want to attract masses of butterflies, try the more reliable options mentioned above.

Painted lady on *Salvia farinacea*

fruit for fliers

Learn how to bring even more butterflies to your landscape.

BY SALLY ROTH

Some butterflies have strange tastes. Instead of nectaring at flowers, lovely creatures like the iridescent red-spotted purple seek out fruits and tree sap. OK, maybe that's not too strange. Fruit juice and sap are sweet treats.

But wait, it gets worse: They also love rotten or fermented fruit, animal waste—and let's not forget sweat! Ever had a butterfly land on your arm or neck on a hot summer day, tickling your skin as it dabs about with its proboscis? Although it may feel like an honor, we're nothing more than a source of sustenance.

To the butterflies, this menu is perfectly natural. Our winged friends need their nourishment in liquid form, and these foods fit the bill.

Offering Nourishment

Most of us won't be adding the more unusual items to our backyard offerings. But setting out fruit is fast and easy, either on a tray, in a tree or in a commercial feeder. Any way you do it, you're almost guaranteed to see some beautiful butterflies that otherwise might not visit your garden.

You'll be amazed at how many butterflies come to a fruit feeder, though you might have to look closely to see them. Fruit-feeding butterflies hold their wings closed when they're eating, and the camouflage-colored undersides look like dead leaves. It's surprisingly easy to overlook even 20 or more guests when they're sitting still.

ROTTEN BLISS. Butterflies will stop by to feed on rotten fruit. Above is a red admiral and at right is a comma butterfly. Both are feeding on some old pears.

Sharing Your Fruit

Start by offering some overripe bananas. Peel back a few strips of skin, and set them on a plate atop a post. Butterflies find them so irresistible, they'll visit your yard for weeks until there's nothing left but dry, blackened peels.

Not all fresh fruit will work, because butterflies can't pierce the skin. But juicy watermelon, cantaloupe and halved oranges will attract butterflies almost instantly. So slice a little bit for you and then a little bit for them!

When it comes to other fruits, the mushier and browner they are, the better. Those signs of decay in peaches, pears and apples show that fermentation is taking place, which boosts the sugars in the fruit and softens the flesh so that it's easy to sip up with a proboscis.

Remember that bees, wasps and fruit flies are likely to come for their share, too, so play it safe and keep your fruit feeder in a discreet spot, away from play areas and paths. If raccoons get grabby, put your fruit in a wire suet cage and hang it out of harm's way.

heavenly color, earthly tastes

Watch for some of these species at your fruit feeder.

Red admiral

Red-spotted purple

Viceroy

Question mark

Comma

Hackberry emperor

Tawny emperor

Mourning cloak

Malachite

Robber fly

Narcissus bulb fly

Bee fly

Tachinid fly

a bee?
or not a bee?

Don't be afraid—most of these flies are harmless and even helpful in your garden.

BY ERIC EATON

Just because it buzzes doesn't mean it's a bee. You may be surprised to learn just how many other insects masquerade as bees, including moths, beetles and the real masters of disguise, flies.

We have a tendency to think of flies as garbage-infesting, picnic-harassing, bloodsucking pests. But actually, most flies are big allies in the yard and garden. Take a look at these bee look-alikes, and find out why you really do want them as permanent backyard guests.

Clever Disguises

It pays to mimic bees. After all, they can sting to defend themselves, and potential predators know this. Birds quickly learn to associate bold patterns of black and yellow, white or red with trouble. Of course, no fly can actually sting, but flies gain protection by looking as if they can.

The most common bee mimics are the hoverflies, members of the Syrphidae family, which resemble small bees or wasps such as yellow jackets. Some even sound like wasps, with the frequency of their wing beats matching that of their stinging counterparts. They are garden friendly, helping to pollinate flowers and eat aphids.

The Asilidae family's robber flies are excellent mimics of bumblebees. Instead of visiting flowers, they perch on foliage, twigs or the ground, and then scan the sky overhead. When another insect flies over, the robber fly zooms off to grab the victim and then returns to its perch. This fly family, too, helps control some of the less desirable garden insects.

Honeybee

Bumblebee

Syrphid fly

TAKE ANOTHER LOOK. Is it a bee or is it a fly? You might be surprised at the results. Most of the pictures on these two pages depict flies, but you wouldn't know it because they do such a good job of mimicking bees. How many of these fliers fooled you?

More Look-Alikes

Bee flies, also called "wanna-bees," are in the Bombyliidae family. Their hairy bodies are delicate and can go bald during their brief lives as adults. Many bee flies have a long proboscis that looks much like a mosquito's bloodsucking snout. No worries—harmless bee flies feed on nectar.

Feather-legged flies in the Tachinidae family really take

their disguise to the next level with imitation pollen baskets on their hind legs. As adults, they may pollinate flowers; as larvae, feather-legged flies are parasitic on stinkbugs and squash bugs.

So the next time you're out in your yard, take a closer look at that bee you notice and see if it's really a fly instead. Either way, chances are it's a helpful insect, not a pest.

bee or fly?

Look for these traits when you're differentiating bees from flies. Don't be afraid to get close. Foraging bees are too intent on what they're doing to bother with you, and (bonus!) flies have no stingers at all.

WINGS
Bees have two pairs of wings, whereas flies have only one set. But since the forewings and hind wings of bees are usually connected, they may appear to have only one pair.

ANTENNAE
Bees have relatively long antennae. Conversely, most flies have very short antennae, with a long bristle called an arista at the tip.

EYES
Both bees and flies have compound eyes that excel at detecting motion, which is why it's so hard to swat them. But flies, unlike bees, have enormous eyes that meet at the top of the head in the male, and nearly so in the female.

MOUTHPARTS
Bees have chewing mouthparts and a tonguelike proboscis. Flies have a spongy pad at the end of a flexible "arm," or a spearlike beak.

BEHAVIOR
Few bees hover, at least for extended periods. Many flies seem to be able to hover indefinitely.

beetles with benefits

Here's why you want to host these helpful little insects.

BY DAVID MIZEJEWSKI

Not all beetles have such fanciful names as fireflies and ladybugs. But many of them have something more important in common: They're good to have in your garden.

Ground beetle

Scarab beetles

Coleoptera, more commonly known as beetles, is the most diverse insect order, with more than 350,000 species—24,000 in North America alone.

So there's a good chance that you're going to encounter beetles in your garden. While it's true that some are pests (Japanese beetles come to mind), many more are a boon to gardeners, pollinating plants, preying on pests or helping to compost decaying plant and animal material.

Remember that if you use toxic pesticides, you often kill off all the helpful insects, too, including beetles. I always say that instead of using chemicals, it's better to have a diversely planted garden that provides lots of habitat for hardworking beetles and other pollinators and predators. Here are some of the most common beneficial beetles in the garden. If you see one, let it be!

Ladybird beetles

Probably the best known group of beetles, they vary in color and pattern. Some are red or orange with black spots, some are black with red spots, while others have no spots at all. All are predatory both as larvae and adults, feeding on soft-bodied plant pests such as aphids, mealybugs, caterpillars and scales.

Rove beetles

These long-bodied beetles look something like earwigs and are found in the same habitat, under rocks, logs and leaf litter. Unlike earwigs, however, rove beetles are predatory.

Soldier beetles

These beetles are active during the day and live in vegetation, where they feed on pollen and nectar and serve as pollinators. They also eat other insects. Their larvae are carnivorous, feeding on eggs and other insect larvae.

Ground beetles

This nocturnal family includes the tiger beetle and bombardier beetle. Most are voracious predators that patrol the ground in search of prey. Their larvae, too, are predatory. Ground beetles are swift runners; many species have large mandibles used to hold and dispatch victims.

Fireflies

Famous for their glowing abdomens, many firefly species don't live long as adults because they are too focused on mating and reproducing to eat, but their larvae are predatory, feasting on other insects, slugs and snails.

Scarab beetles

Many species of this group of stout, oval-shaped beetles feed on animal dung, and for that we should certainly thank them.

Soldier beetles

Rove beetle

Firefly

year-round butterflies

BY KENN KAUFMAN

Painted lady

SPRING *Keep an eye out for these early fliers.*

Spring's arrival is hard to pin down on a calendar, but all over North America, butterflies mark the unfolding season.

Springtime Specialties

In the southernmost United States, winter fades almost imperceptibly into spring. Elsewhere, however, particular butterflies are sure signs of springtime: They don't fly at any other time of year. Among these are small white butterflies such as West Virginia and spring whites, and various types of orangetips and marbles. Their caterpillars feed on wild plants in the mustard family, which grow mainly in spring. The adult butterflies must emerge early so females can lay eggs and the caterpillars can feed while the plants are available.

Other spring specialties include certain tiny blue butterflies, such as the spring azure and the silvery blue. These gems may show up in gardens, or they may gather by the dozens around the edges of mud puddles. Less noticeable are some small, dark butterflies in the hairstreak and skipper families—they're somewhat obscure, but worth seeking out for their poetic names, such as frosted elfin or

sleepy duskywing. But no one is likely to overlook some of the big swallowtails that start flying early in the season, such as the gorgeous, streamer-winged zebra swallowtail.

Returning North

Early in spring, monarch butterflies that had spent the winter in Mexico will begin to move north or northeast, eventually crossing into Texas. At some point, the females will stop to lay eggs on milkweed plants, launching another generation that continues the journey north. Before the end of May, the vanguard of the migrants reaches the Great Lakes or even southern Canada.

A few others—red admirals, painted ladies and American ladies among them—are on the move, too, though not in such an organized or predictable way. In the Southwest, tens of thousands of painted ladies may take part in a mass flight, flooding into gardens along their path.

Week by week, as the season advances, new types of butterflies emerge: bright yellow sulphurs, subtle brown satyrs, flashy orange fritillaries and others, each adding to the palette of colors that graces gardens in summer.

SUMMER

This time of year, flying jewels are everywhere.

From the fringes of the tropics to the Arctic, summer is high season for North American butterflies.

Learning the Life Cycle

A large, diverse garden may be alive with butterflies all summer long. If we watch casually, it might seem that we're seeing the same ones throughout the season, but the reality is more complicated and interesting.

Most adult butterflies live two or three weeks at most. If we see the same kinds all summer, we may be observing more than one generation. With small butterflies like pearl crescents or tailed blues, the first females in spring or early summer lay eggs that soon hatch, the caterpillars grow rapidly and pupate, and another batch of adults emerges; there may be three or more generations during the warmer months. The populations of these species may seem to rise and fall during the season, with numbers of adults dwindling before the next brood emerges.

As we might expect, the number of generations is fewer in regions where the summer is shorter. Several kinds of butterflies, such as some swallowtails, may have several broods per year in the Deep South but only one in the North. And some have a single generation per year, regardless of latitude.

Regional Standouts

In the cold climates of Arctic Canada and Alaska, a few remarkable butterflies—mostly lesser fritillaries and satyrs—fly every other year. Summers are so short that the caterpillars hatch in one season, hibernate through winter, feed and grow through the next summer, then hibernate through a second winter before pupating and emerging as adults that summer. Butterfly watchers who travel to the tundra might be puzzled to find that a species could be common one summer and seemingly absent the next.

At the opposite climate extreme, southern butterflies push northward in summer. Tropical sulphurs and skippers may move from Mexico into the American Southwest; widespread butterflies like buckeyes and red admirals may move north past the Great Lakes. By the end of summer, migratory monarchs have reached their northern point, far into Canada, and are poised for fall when they drift south.

Common buckeye

Monarch

AUTUMN

How butterflies prepare for the cooler days ahead.

For most North American butterflies, autumn is less a distinct season than a long goodbye to summer, with its bountiful fields and gardens, before the onset of winter.

Promising a Future

Most adult butterflies will perish before winter arrives. Long before the bitter cold sets in, females laid eggs, ensuring a generation for the following year. With that responsibility done, the adults may live out the rest of their short lives wandering in a seemingly aimless way. However, a few kinds of butterflies live through the winter as adults, hibernating in sheltered sites, and these may be actively seeking such roosting spots as the fall advances. Mourning cloaks, question marks, commas and tortoiseshells are among these hibernators, so if we see them near woodpiles or tree cavities, they are likely scouting out winter shelter.

A few kinds of butterflies have their only flight period of the year in late summer and fall. The red-bordered satyr, which flaps floppily through southwestern canyons in September, is one; another is Leonard's skipper, a sharply marked denizen of northeastern meadows. However, most of these fall fliers are unlikely to show up in gardens, and are unfamiliar to most people. So the majority of the butterfly activity that we see in fall will be a continuation of summer behavior—including the northward push of southern species. Subtropical creatures such as big, pale cloudless sulphurs and orange fiery skippers may still be flying north in early October, even into southern Canada.

Taking Flight

Butterflies' most distinctive fall movement is monarchs' southward flight. In spring and summer, multiple generations gradually move north, away from Mexico and coastal California wintering grounds. A new generation of adults that emerges in early fall has a different instinct: to fly south. At places like Point Pelee, Ontario, monarchs may gather en masse to roost at night before continuing their amazing journey. Through a kind of inherited memory that is as mysterious as it is notable, they will somehow "return" to the same wintering sites that their great-great-grandparents left months earlier. We may not understand how they do it, but we can enjoy the spectacle.

WINTER
What are butterflies up to at the chilliest time of year?

In a few regions of North America, winter's effect is scarcely felt, and there, butterfly-watching may be exciting all year. At the southern tips of Texas and Florida, for example, gardens may be alive with butterflies throughout January and February, unless they are knocked back by the rare hard freeze. But away from these subtropical zones, winter marks the low ebb for butterfly activity.

Time to Recharge

Along the Gulf of Mexico, in the lowlands of the desert southwest, and in the Mediterranean climates of coastal California, mild winters allow some butterflies to continue flying through the season. They may be resting out of sight on cooler, cloudy days, but red admirals, painted ladies, some sulphurs and others take wing on warm, sunny days, regardless of what the calendar says.

East of the Rocky Mountains, most monarchs are absent, wintering in the mountains of Mexico. However, much of the western population spends the season along the California coast. The monarchs are sedentary, hanging in dense clusters in their tall roost trees most of the time. Occasionally, however, especially on the warmest days,

they scatter to the wind like orange confetti, drifting back to the roost at the approach of evening.

Surviving the Cold

The monarch migration is famous but also unique: No other butterfly has such a precise migratory pattern, and few migrate at all. So when we don't see butterflies in winter, they are not necessarily gone, merely out of sight. They may survive the coldest months in any of their four major life stages: egg, caterpillar (larva), pupa (chrysalis) or adult.

A few tough butterflies hibernate as adults, sleeping in sheltered crevices. A February thaw may awaken them, leading to the startling sight of a mourning cloak, comma or tortoiseshell flying over snowdrifts. Others, such as some swallowtails, spend the winter as pupae, ready to emerge as adults in spring. A few more overwinter in the egg stage.

Caterpillars might seem more vulnerable, but the majority of our butterflies do spend the winter in that form. They may actually hatch in fall and not begin to eat until spring. So even in northern midwinter, when the land is locked in ice and snow, next summer's butterflies are represented by myriad tiny caterpillars sleeping in the cold.

Mourning cloak

butterfly cafe BY ALISON AUTH

Invite winged wonders to dine in style.

supplies

- Old chandelier with chain
- Screwdrivers (both types)
- Needle-nose pliers
- Spray primer and paint
- Overripe fruit
- Sand (optional)
- Water (optional)

Yes, a feeder will attract butterflies! Overripe fruit placed in a dish of damp sand (to serve as a moat to keep ants away) is a simple makeshift butterfly feeder. But don't stop there—get a little creative about where you set up shop. For instance, how about a chandelier?

STEP 1. Pick up a cheap chandelier at a thrift store or garage sale. Once you've settled on your chandelier choice, you need to deconstruct it. Cut the wires as needed and pull out the bulb sockets, wires and any other electrical parts. Each fixture will have its own quirks, but your mission is to expose the "cups" for the fruit.

STEP 2. Once you have stripped the chandelier of all its unnecessary parts, wash it off and let it dry. Remember that paint adheres to clean surfaces much better than to dusty or dirty ones.

STEP 3. Time to paint! Instant transformation in a can—is anything better? For greater longevity, definitely use a spray primer first. And remember to block out your painting time so that you can do quick successive coats within minutes of each other.

STEP 4. After your chandelier is painted and dry, it is ready for hanging. Choose a location that's accessible for refilling.

STEP 5. Put out the yum-yums! We used pineapple and strawberry kabobs, but whatever is handy and past its prime is the rule.

STEP 6. If you want to make the sand moats, pack the "saucers" of the chandelier with sand and slowly pour water over the sand. If you have some little river rocks or pebbles, tuck them into the sand for a sweet butterfly landing spot.

STEP 7. Grab a slice or two of fresh fruit for yourself and settle in for a season of watching happy butterflies!

just add fruit!

TRY THIS! Fruit isn't the only thing you can put out for butterflies. Other ingredients such as molasses, brown sugar, Gatorade and stale beer can be used at your discretion. Use what's handy and experiment away!

Bee in a hollyhock
Photo by Justus de Cuveland / Getty Images

South Dakota flutter
Semifinalist in our
Backyard Photo Contest
Photo by Cheryl Walberg

Butterflies
Photo by Cathy Keifer /
Shutterstock.com

Swallowtail in a daylily
Photo by Carol Lynne Fowler

Moth on yarrow
Photo by Emjay Smith / Shutterstock.com

Index

A

B

C

Index

"*If one truly loves nature, one finds beauty everywhere.*"

—Vincent van Gogh